Résumé Writing

A COMPREHENSIVE HOW-TO-DO-IT GUIDE

Burdette E. Bostwick

The B. E. Bostwick Company
Management Consultants

A WILEY-INTERSCIENCE PUBLICATION

JOHN WILEY & SONS, New York • Chichester • Brisbane • Toronto

Library of Congress Cataloging in Publication Data:

Bostwick, Burdette E
  Résumé writing.

  "A Wiley-Interscience publication."
  Includes indexes.
    1. Résumés (Employment)—Handbooks, manuals, etc.
  2. Applications for positions—Handbooks, manuals,
etc. I. Title.

HF5383.B57   650'.14   75-45306
ISBN 0-471-09060-3

Printed in the United States of American

10 9 8

To my wife Betty
for her courage and understanding

Preface

This book is intended to help in preparing superior résumés, be they simple or complex. Who needs résumés? Almost all job seekers do. Nearly 90% of the "want ads" for management and professional personnel—either entry positions or positions paying more than $12,000 a year—call for a résumé. Your chances of getting a job or the kind of job you want are thus about 90% smaller if you lack one. Furthermore, the only entrée into the 80% of available positions that are never advertised is by way of a résumé.

A résumé, while not guaranteering a job, does, if properly written, open the door to an interview. It can affirmatively affect the decision to hire. Your résumé is the costume, the arrangement, and the libretto; your interview is the lyrics and the interpretation of your role.

Whether you are unemployed, seek a new career, are restless in present employment, wish to test your marketability, or plan to move to greener pastures, your résumé can, literally or figuratively, be your magic carpet. A résumé is the best and perhaps only way of widely disseminating important job information about yourself.

Surveys of résumé users, as you will see, suggest a direct relation between résumé use and the length of time needed to climb the executive ladder to success. Just as a picture is worth a thousand words, so a good résumé speaks eloquently for itself. Most of the many examples included in this book (see The Index of Résumés) are based on actual résumés, with names and other data changed sufficiently to avoid identification. They were selected because of their success in getting interviews or jobs. All were described as effective by the individuals themselves. At least one of the résumés was strongly influential in placing a candidate in a position paying more than $75,000 a year. Instead of being contrived, hence forced and artificial, these résumés are human and have the ring of reality.

Although the book is intended for all job seekers, management résumé preparation is stressed. The complexity of résumé preparation grows with job responsibilities. The situation proceeds from "what can I write about myself?" to "What can I leave out?"

This book is a distillation of many years of résumé study to find the best forms and methods of expression and of many years of management experience with people and jobs of all kinds. I have written more than a thousand résumés and read thousands more. None is or can be perfect—for lack of the conjunction of the perfect person with the perfect writer at the perfect time. Superior craftsmanship can be attained, however.

Résumés take various forms, some of which experience has shown to be better than others. Moreover, their content has proved to be more important than any form. Your prize for writing a better résumé might be increased income, higher achievement, and greater happiness.

BURDETTE E. BOSTWICK

New York, New York
February 1976

Contents

Illustrations

The data analyzed and reported in this book are taken from a sampling of 1000 résumés in my own files. They reflect confidential information given to me for résumé preparation by individuals in more than 60 employment classifications. To my knowledge, such data have never before been systematized and analyzed. There may well be a bias toward upper and middle management. Those entering the job market may be underrepresented in the data reported here, since they would be concentrated among the 80% of job seekers who write their own résumés. Nevertheless, the charts disclose significant and interesting facts about the persons who prepare résumés. By scientific polling standards a sample of 1000 is amply sufficient for valid conclusions.

What Is a Résumé

A résumé is your personal advertisement. It is the most widely accepted medium of communication between a job seeker and a prospective employer. It differs from an ordinary advertisement in that it is not directed to the general public, but to the employer. An employer may receive hundreds of résumés for a single position. If you wish to be one of the few selected for an interview, you must make your résumé superior to the common run.

Writing a résumé is not an easy task, though it is a very important one in terms of personal reward. The difficulty lies in organization and objectivity. It is not as natural to write about yourself as it is to write about a place, an event, or even another person. There are relatively few great autobiographies! At least 70% of the résumés I have read are deficient in some respect. You can make yours a superior document by studying the method of its preparation.

The résumé, crucial in getting an interview, may enter the final decision to hire. Its role is increasing because of more intense competition for jobs and possibly slower job growth as capital formation is restricted and corporations and institutions learn to live without less productive and less necessary employees.

You can use this book in two ways. Preferably you can learn to write an effective résumé, stamped with your own hallmark. Or, possibly, you can preempt one of the résumé examples as a model for your own résumé, though it might then appear "canned." You need not master all of the résumé styles—they are included to show the options. Pick the one best suited to you.

The words *chronological* and *functional* occur frequently in this book. *Chronological* here refers to the arrangement of data in the order of time of occurrence, but, unlike in a biography or history, the order is reversed. That is, in a résumé the most recent experience is described first and older experiences last. (See the résumé on p. 37.)

Thus the main body of our résumé called *Chronological Résumé with Summary Page* (see Section 14, p. 43), starting with the second page, is chronological. The *summary page* is a brief interpretation of the *succeeding* pages. It is written last but placed first in the completed résumé.

The word *functional* refers to a style of résumé that describes activities in each area of experience separately without reference to the companies for which the function was performed or to the time of performance. For example:

EXPERIENCE

GENERAL   Held P. & L. responsibility for $10 million division.
MANAGER   Reorganized production and cost accounting depart-
                 ments. Reduced costs. Set up new marketing strategies.
                 Increased sales. Also consolidated two manufacturing
                 plants for improved efficiency.

MARKETING   Surveyed market for power tools. Established share of
MANAGEMENT   market goals for each territory; assigned quotas; installed
                 new salesmen's compensation plan. Redirected advertis-
                 ing. Increased sales 36% within 2 years for one company,
                 23% for another company and 10% for a third.

EMPLOYMENT HISTORY

A.B.C. Company, Chicago, Ill.
D.E.F. Company, Portland, Me.
X.Y.Z. Company, Newark, N.J.

These experiences (described in summary form here) might apply to one,
two, or all three of the companies.

Brief descriptions of the various résumé styles, together with our recommendations, are given below. Detailed analyses appear later.

1. **Basic Résumé.** The best form for one entering the job market or having very limited experience. (See Section 12, p. 25.)
2. **Chronological Résumé.** The second best form (sometimes the best)
   for a middle or upper management executive, since it permits the
   sharpest delineation of accomplishments. (See Section 13, p. 34.)
3. **Chronological Résumé with Summary Page.** The best form for a middle or upper management executive—in addition to permitting a clear
   listing of accomplishments, it also contains a *Summary Page*. (See
   Section 14, p. 42.)
4. **Functional Résumé.** An excellent form, especially for one with
   experience in several job functions, such as marketing, finance, and
   general management. A preferred form for educators at the administrative level. Some personnel executives profess a liking for this form.
   (See Section 15, p. 57.)

5. **Functional-by-Company (or Institution) Résumé.** Advantageously associates function with the company for which it was performed, but loses the impact of the pure *Functional Résumé.* (See Section 16, p. 63.)
6. **Harvard Résumé.** Has an excellent appearance, but less effective, from both the job seeker's and the employer's point of view, than the styles discussed so far. (See Section 17, p. 71.)
7. **Creative Résumé.** For special uses only. Has no definite structure. (See Section 18, p. 76.)
8. **Narrative Résumé.** A specialized form that may serve well in situations deviating from the norm. (See Section 19, p. 78.)
9. **Professional Résumé.** For lawyers, doctors, teachers, and other professionals whose education and accreditation are of primary importance to the reader. (See Section 20, p. 82.)
10. **Accomplishment Résumé.** Not generally recommended because its raison d'ètre is to obscure. (See Section 21, p. 89.)

These evaluations are based on personal opinions and on experience.

The selection of a résumé form may also change with your career. You might start with the *Basic Résumé,* graduate after a few years to the *Chronological Résumé,* and finally proceed to the *Chronological Résumé with Summary Page* or to the *Functional Résumé.*

A *covering* letter is an essential short introduction to a résumé. Of the samples included in this book there will be one more "right" for you than any of the others, which you can then amend to fit your circumstances. A *broadcast* letter—different from a résumé and a covering letter—is also fully explained.

The word *résumé* (from the Latin resūmere, "to take up again," and the French résumer, "to resume, summarize"), pronounced ráy zū māy, is defined *by Webster's Third International Dictionary* as "a short account of one's career and qualifications prepared typically by an applicant for a position." Sometimes the term *curriculum vitae,* pronounced ka rick' you lum vi tēe, is used. A résumé can also be defined in a number of other ways:

1. A résumé is an essential part of a job search at the managerial level.
2. A résumé, or the tools that derive from it, is the most effective instrument for finding work or for gaining one's desired vocational situation.
3. A résumé is a door opener to an interview.
4. A résumé is a formal document describing the qualifications of a job seeker.

5. A résumé is a self-appraisal that stresses past and present accomplishments in order to indicate future potential.
6. A résumé is a tool for self-evaluation which, when completed, may suggest new steps toward the attainment of goals.
7. A résumé is a brief business biography or vocational history that emphasizes experience, accomplishment, education, and objectives expressed in favorable terms.

HELP WANTED DISPLAY ADVERTISING

A survey of 1000 "help-wanted," "positions available" advertisements in *The New York Times* (Sunday) and *The Wall Street Journal* was conducted over a period of 5 to 6 weeks in February and March of 1975. The results were as follows:

1.	Ask for résumé specifically	757
2.	Ask for reply with full details (probably requiring résumé)	118
3.	Ask for reply only	74
4.	Ask for reply by telephone	51
	Total	1000

Items 1 and 2, involving résumés, came to 87.5%. Adding item 3, for which a résumé would be the most appropriate reply, we find 94.5% of the advertisements to be résumé related.

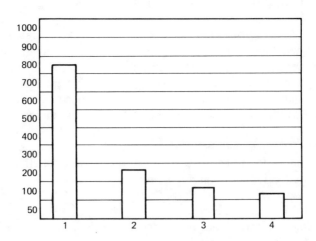

S E C T I O N   2

Who Uses Résumés

Almost every job seeker—whether unemployed or wishing to change positions—needs a résumé. Résumés are prepared by persons at all levels of employment: judges, lawyers, cabinet members, managers, chief executive of-

RÉSUMÉ USERS: BY AGE GROUP

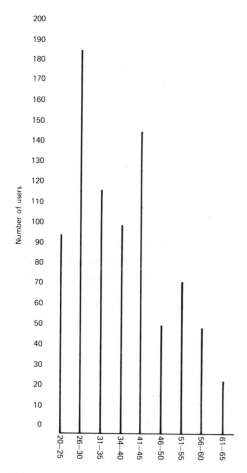

As would be expected, the greatest inci-
dence of résumé use is in the age group
from 26 to 45 years (533). The most
frequent users are between the ages of 26
and 30; those between 41 and 45 are
next. Most of those in the age group 20
to 25 are new to the job market. (From a
sample of 1000, of whom 799 gave ages.)

ficers, administrators, bookkeepers, secretaries. In my experience and according to surveys, most résumés are prepared by those looking for management, professional, or performing arts positions. Résumés are not usually required for clerical and skilled labor jobs, though their wider use might possibly expand and upgrade job opportunities in these areas. The only individuals who do not need résumés are those whose outstanding careers make it unnecessary for them to seek jobs—rather, jobs seek them. (See pp. 5, 7, 10, and 16.)

S E C T I O N   3

Why Write a Résumé

A résumé serves to introduce you to the employer and help gain a personal interview. You need a résumé because for most advertised *management* jobs (see p. 4) a resume is required before an interview will be granted. Employers require résumés because they are executive time-savers. A personal interview takes hours; a résumé can be read in a few minutes.

There are other reasons for writing a résumé:

1. A résumé forms the basis for a mail campaign about yourself, using either the actual résumé or a summary of it in the form of a broadcast letter. The 80% of available jobs that are never advertised must be sought by mail.
2. A résumé can be used to test your marketability while you remain safely employed.
3. A résumé helps you to organize the facts of your past accomplishments, clarifying what you can or wish to do in the future. Many advisors recommend that a résumé be updated every six months or once a year. You thus remain continuously aware of your progress, or lack of it, and of your up-to-the minute responsibilities and achievements. What you did last year may have lost importance by reason of newer accomplishments.

4. A résumé in expanded form may help gain academic credits for "life work," an important opportunity offered by many universities.
5. A résumé may be utilized in buying a business to impart information about yourself to the seller.
6. A résumé can serve to solicit business if you are, for example, a consultant, a freelance artist or writer, or a part-time worker. A more elaborate brochure explaining your qualifications can be based on it.
7. A résumé prepares you for your job interview by forcing you to think about and express yourself in an organized way. A résumé is your personal guidance manual for speaking about yourself fluently and unhesitatingly.

RÉSUMÉ USERS: MEN AND WOMEN

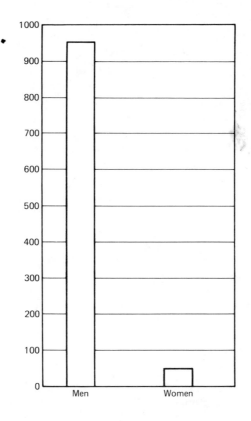

S E C T I O N   4

The Nature of the Résumé

A résumé is a sales presentation of yourself. It should not be a mere detailing of past job experiences. It must be alive and interesting and must present your accomplishments to the maximum degree. Make it a portrait in color, rather than a black-and-white photograph. Will it favorably differentiate you from other applicants for the position? The reader of your résumé should be able to infer from your past achievements your expected contributions in a new position. The résumé should be honest—do not inflate your abilities beyond your capacity to produce.

There are many characteristics that make people come alive as individuals—different from the crowd. Accomplishments also can be avocational and interesting to mention. In what ways you are equipping yourself for greater responsibilities in the future is of interest. Your attitudes toward current events might find a brief place in your résumé or covering letter. Political involvement outside your business life can be mentioned if not too controversial. Participation in scouting, your church, your community, your children's school, as an alumnus of your own school or college, successful fund raising, and other activities can be utilized to generate interest if vocational material is inadequate.

S E C T I O N   5

A Good Résumé— A Must

To get a job you need not be superior to other applicants; few would have jobs if only ideal applicants were hired! However your résumé should make you appear to be superior. An employer may receive hundreds of résumés for one position. A large corporation may handle 50,000 or more résumés a year. You can improve your chance of being one of the few selected for an interview by studying how to prepare your résumé; a study relatively free of competition and likely to bring great rewards.

In actual fact, you may be superior to other applicants but no one will know it unless you get a chance to explain your qualifications in a personal interview. Words in writing are different from the spoken word. It would be normal for what you say about yourself in writing to seem better to you and to be better, than what you have ever been able to say about yourself orally. This is because in writing about yourself you have had to think more clearly. The chore of writing down, by itself, demands clearer exposition. In a conversation you can repeat yourself or erase previous errors in a succeeding statement. What appears in writing cannot be changed. This also underscores again how important a résumé can be in helping you to express yourself properly during an interview.

The importance of résumés grows daily because of the increased competition for jobs caused by an ever larger population increasingly better educated and better qualified.

SECTION 6
Résumé Length

There is no standard résumé length. A résumé should be as long as it needs to be to present important information concisely and interestingly. Successful résumés have been as short as one page and as long as six pages. It is conciseness, relevance, and interest that matter. A six page résumé can be concise; a three page résumé, verbose.

For example, there are many individuals who have extensive achievements over a period of 20 or 25 years or more. Achievements follow patterns. Some résumés could almost be textbooks for others to follow in climbing the ladder to organizational success. Of course they must include a personal method of expression and word usage to avoid textbook dullness. The point is that one can hardly compress a lifetime of achievement into a page of writing. Most employers of upper level managers are interested in what you have done if it has been well done.

If you are a Henry Ford, a Lynn Townsend, a Henry Kissinger you will not need to write much; but if you are not widely known you must explain yourself. There is a happy balance between too much and too little.

The search for a perfect résumé will never end. A perfect résumé is almost impossible, but the following would be:

To Whom it May Concern:
    Available.
        William Shakespeare

RÉSUMÉ USERS: BY JOB CLASSIFICATION

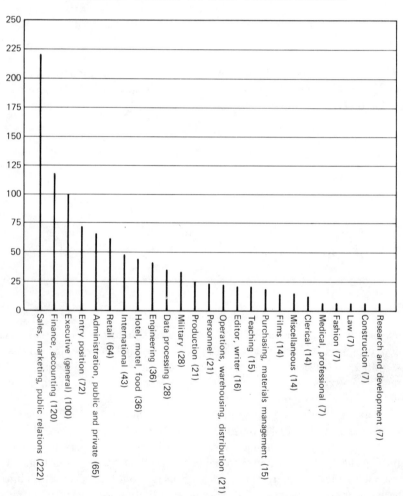

The greatest resume use occurs in sales, marketing, and public relations. Persons employed in these areas may be more accustomed to writing, more aware of the benefits of advertising, or perhaps merely more restless than are other groups. (From a sample of 1000.)

SECTION 7
Résumé Language

The language of a résumé must be succinct, crisp, trenchant, expressive, interesting, and personal. Words, phrases, sentences, and paragraphs illustrating this type of writing appear later in this book (Appendix B). Use the specialized vocabulary of your job area. Scientists, data processors, lawyers, financial people, economists, engineers, social workers—each specialization has its own nomenclature. However, a résumé must never be so technical that those outside your discipline fail to understand it. If you have experience in a vocation, your language will naturally reflect it. If you have little or no experience, ignore this aspect.

There are more languages or dialects in English than you might think. To name just a few: academic, conversational, vernacular, bureaucratic, poetic, formal, jargon, argot, Gullah. They arise from education or lack of it, from environmental exposure, from the desire to confuse, from the combined use of two or more other languages to supplement English.

The fact of a résumé language arises out of a need for clear expression in a minimum number of words to create a maximum impact. There is no time for relaxed prose. The average résumé must make its *impression* in 20 to 30 seconds. If the first impression is good the entire résumé will be read. If the first impression is poor, it will be discarded. Average reading time is about four words per second.

There is the hope to lend excitement and create an urgency to make a decision. Most of all, there is the need of discipline to attain your objective which dictates the "language" or mode of expression.

SECTION 8
Common Résumé Faults

In my experience, the nine résumé deficiencies listed below are the most common ones and should be guarded against when writing a résumé.

1. A mere listing of the positions you have held, without further explanation.
2. Failure to state your objective early in the résumé.
3. Failure to describe your accomplishments.
4. Stating an objective for which you are unqualified.
5. Omitting a description of your responsibilities in the positions held.
6. Wordiness, incorrect spelling, and bad grammar.
7. Incomplete vocational history.
8. Omission of vital statistics (except for reasons discussed later).
9. Poor physical appearance.

S E C T I O N   9

The Elements of a
Résumé

WHAT TO OMIT

The following information is usually best omitted from your résumé:

1. Omit date. Your résumé should remain current for an extended period of time. Place the date in your covering letter.
2. Omit race, religion, political affiliation, and the like, unless part of the main thrust of your résumé. Though the law forbids discrimination for such reasons, you should not offer them as a basis for selection, which you do if you include them in the résumé. Disregard this advice if you know your prospective employer to be partial to certain kinds of people. Thus a Catholic parish would not only employ a Catholic priest rather than a Baptist minister, but might also tend to hire Catholic clerical workers—a tendency that holds equally for any religious institution.
3. Omit matters that are negative, detrimental, or awkward to write about.

4. Omit salary requirements.

- A leading reason for seeking new employment is to improve compensation. Avoid being restricted by your past salary level.
- You are entitled to the income level of the position being offered. The company should indicate what it is prepared to pay.
- Salary is negotiable—based on the nature of the position and your expected contribution to it.
- It is unwise to commit yourself to a salary level before the interview because you might underrate your potential.
- In the same way a salary that the employer finds unacceptable from a mere reading of your résumé (causing the résumé to be discarded) might become acceptable after the interview.

    Some qualifications are in order, however. If an advertisement asks for salary information, you might supply it. Write it in by hand at the end of the résumé, together with bonuses and fringe benefits, if substantial, or combine all in an inclusive lump sum. I am ambivalent about this. In a very strong résumé salary disclosure can probably be avoided even when specifically requested.

    Furthermore, very significant salary growth—from $12,000 to $40,000 within a short time—shows that your employer has recognized your merits in the most important possible way, and this in turn indicates strong functional progress. In such a case, making salary data known, showing your salary growth by percentages or graphically, is another way of buttressing your accomplishments.

    Finally, if your earnings are or have been at a certain level that you are confident you can match in your new position, you might safely include your income expectancy in your covering letter.

5. Omit references.

- An employer should have no interest in your references until after he has become interested in you—after the interview.
- A prospective employer might consult the persons given as references before interviewing you. This is undesirable because you wish to be the first one to describe yourself.
- Persons named as references can become irritated by too many calls.
- You will not wish to have your present employer called as a reference before employment interest in you has been indicated.

However, any extraordinary references that you might have can be included. Extraordinary references would include famous people, individuals of stature in your area of competence, important political figures, and the like.

MAGNITUDE OF RÉSUMÉ USE: A SPECULATION

The New York Times and *The Wall Street Journal* carry about 250 display "jobs available" advertisements each week. Assuming that these "bibles" of the job market account for 10% of all management jobs advertised throughout the country, 2500 jobs are listed weekly, 130,000 annually. If advertised jobs reflect only 20% of available positions, there are about 12,500 openings each week or about 650,000 each year. Each of the advertised openings must attract at least 10 résumés, or 1,300,000. Some of these résumés are sent by the same people in answer to several different advertisements; so reduce by half to 650,000. In addition, 200 leading companies receive 25,000 a year (a few as many as 50,000) sent by 125 to 200 writers. Another 2800 companies receive 1000 a year, (2,800,000 résumés) sent by 28,000 writers. Dun and Bradstreet list 67,000 additional companies in the million-dollar and middle-market categories which may receive a number of résumés each year; assume two. Add to these the résumés circulated by new graduates just entering the job market to bring the total to more than 1,000,000. About 1% may be prepared professionally.

A sampling of about 2000 résumés found 80 to 90% of them to be deficient in one or more respects, doing the subject less than justice.

WHAT TO INCLUDE

The elements to be included in résumés are discussed below. The starred items are those essential to any résumé.

*1. **Your personal directory.** Name, address (with zip code), and telephone number (with area code) are obvious essentials that must appear in your résumé. The only exception is the case in which the employer is dealt with by way of an intermediary for reasons of confidentiality. The third party approach is of course less effective than the direct approach and should not be used without good cause. Make sure that the intermediary disclaims any right to compensation for services rendered.

If you are employed, list your business telephone number, provided that privacy of conversation is possible. Repeated unanswered calls to an applicant's home may negatively affect the prospective employer's interest. Immediate availability can be crucial in the decision to hire.

*2. **Objective.** Your résumé should be geared to your job objective. State the objective clearly at the outset. If you know the experience and qualifications needed for a job, direct your résumé to describing, as specifically as possible, your ability to meet the criteria. Most applicants lack such information, which sometimes can be obtained from friends, acquaintances, bankers, competitors, annual company reports, and similar sources. Usually, however a résumé is intended to meet the qualifications of more than one specific job and must be written more broadly. Among the objectives toward which a résumé can be directed are the following:

- An entry position in marketing, finance, or production.
- A management position in marketing, finance, or production, or in any subdivision of these functions.
- A career change—from a profession to business, from military service to business, and the like.
- An office administrative position.

These are general categories. For your résumé choose as specific a job classification as possible from the thousands of categories in existence. A prospective employer should not have to guess what kind of a job you want.

3. **Qualifications: A brief summary, a paragraph long summary, or an expanded full page summary.** Having stated your job objective, you must present your qualifications for it. Qualifications include courses of study, past work experience, and even character traits that can be supported:

- *Ambition* can be indicated by having worked one's way through college.
- *Motivation* can be manifested by having achieved good grades.
- *Commitment* can be shown by a long term ambition to pursue one's objective and enrollment in training toward that end.
- *Intelligence* might be indicated by a high class standing and receipt of awards.

If you have substantial work experience, a summary page is in order. The method of preparing such a page is explained later.

You can describe your qualifications either objectively or subjectively. Allowing your personality to come through will add warmth to an otherwise sterile document, especially if the résumé is short. Objective evaluations can come from official reports on personnel, such as those used by the armed forces and increasingly by many private companies that review their personnel annually, making the results available to the employee.

RÉSUMÉ USERS: EMPLOYED AND UNEMPLOYED

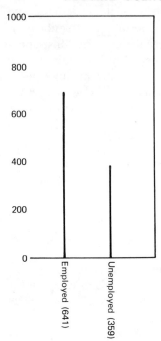

Those who are employed use résumés almost twice as much as do the unemployed. (From a sample of 1000.)

*4. **Experience.** In describing your experience give the dates on which you began and terminated the job. Use the phrase "to present" to indicate current employment. State the name and location of the company, except when present employment must be kept confidential. "Name of Company on Request" may suffice in such cases. It is not necessary to include a company's street address. Describe briefly what the company makes, sells, or does, how large it is, and how many employees it has.

Then list your responsibilities at the company. Use the company's job description of your position or create your own. A corporate job description can be a formidable and necessarily tedious document. Extract from it the highlights of your responsibilities, using key words and sentences, to avoid burdening your résumé with unneeded, though technically relevant, verbiage.

The description of responsibilities should always be followed by a statement of accomplishments. For example:

Responsible for planning entry of Company into chain store distribution. Accomplishments: developed program, hired salesmen, implemented program, contributed new volume of $1 million in first year of operation.

Responsible for transcribing dictation from three advertising agency account executives. Accomplishments: became expert with IBM Executive typewriter; increased typing speed from 50 to 75 words per minute; increased accuracy to 97%.

What you are responsible for doing takes on significance when you describe what you did about it. Ask yourself, "What needed to be done, and what did I do? What happened as a result?"

Follow methodology described for each position you have held in a company and for each company you have worked for. Describe your experience first in chronological sequence; if another style is preferred, rearrange the items later.

*5. **Education.** As a rule education appears near the beginning of a résumé if one has no work experience, and after experience when experience begins to outweigh education after a year or so in a job. One exception is the *Professional Résumé* for reasons explained later.

An academic degree or attendance at a college makes any mention of graduation from high school superflous, though you might wish to list a "name" preparatory school. The high school graduate who did not go to college must mention the fact of graduation. The noncollege graduate should deemphasize education as early as possible in the résumé. Any continuation of education should be noted and described, regardless of the level.

Show your class standing if it is high; otherwise omit it. Mention the honors, awards, and scholarships you have earned.

If your education or individual courses you have attended are particularly relevant to your objective, say so in your résumé (this will be self-evident in the *Professional Résumé*). Advanced degrees should be stated. At this writing a master's degree in business administration (M.B.A.) is the most valuable business degree and commands a compensation advantage of $2000 or more annually. For the nonprofessional a doctoral degree is an advantage if related to the job objective. It is an asset for a researcher, teacher, scientist, writer, and public administrator.

6. **Extracurricular activities.** Listing extensive extracurricular activities can add flavor to a résumé. Omit them if they are few, however, and after you have gained substantial work experience—their significance tends to erode with time. Do list teaching assistantships, tutoring, waiting on tables, elective student organization offices, sports participation, school newspaper experience, and special distinctions of any kind. They enable the employer to know you better and may strike a responsive chord that might provide an edge in selection for employment.

7. **Summer work while attending school or college.** Employers look with favor on those who have used their school or college holidays for constructive activities. Therefore, summer employment is a worthwhile addition to a résumé, and so is having partially or wholly worked one's way through college. This entry in the résumé is a character building block.

8. **Military service.** Your service in the armed forces, with an honorable discharge, has a place in your résumé. Usually its mention should be brief. Extended description is in order, however, if military service forms a major part of your background—the young man who has been in the armed forces for two to five or more years and has no other employment experience or the career military man who seeks a new career after retirement from the service. Your service record supplies a wealth of information from which interesting, persuasive, and relevant material can be drawn as the basis for a highly effective résumé presentation. Take care to avoid an overlong discussion of your military career, no matter how extensive—stress the factors most relevant to your civilian job objective.

9. **Professional membership.** Membership in professional and trade associations denotes an ongoing interest in expanding one's vocational experience. Some memberships are almost mandatory for certain job classifications. Any industrially, commercially, or professionally recognized membership should be listed in your résumé.

10. **Community activities.** Some companies, highly conscious of their local image, favor employee participation in fund drives, charitable board memberships, and community assistance activities. Participation in community activities may characterize you in the eyes of a potential employer as an individual with broad interests and the potential for greater managerial responsibilities.

11. **Accreditations and licenses.** Include all accreditations and licenses related to your vocation in your résumé. Examples are C.P.A., C.L.U., Licensed Engineer, Licensed Real Estate Broker, and R.N. Honorary degrees should also be listed.

12. **Patents and publications.** Patents, particularly important to the research scientist, the R.&D. manager or employee, and the engineer, as indicators of original thinking should always be included in a résumé. Publication carries special weight in teaching, business consulting, law, and other professions. They serve as tools in evaluating you, and as a basis for a constructive and interesting interview.

*13. **Personal data.** Personal data are date of birth, marital status, sex (if name is ambiguous), state of health (if excellent), citizenship (if potentially unclear), number of children, home ownership, willingness to relocate, geographical employment preference (if any), availability for employment (if not immediate), extensive travel experience, height, and weight.

The laws relating to equal opportunity employment make it illegal for an employer to discriminate by reasons of age, color, creed, race, religion, and sex. You must judge for yourself whether to include all these data in your résumé. Give age if you are young; omit it if you are over 50. On the other hand, if no age is given, the employer may infer more years than the actual number. Approximate age can be guessed quite accurately from dates of graduation and from the length of your career. You might also consider excluding all dates from your résumé. Age is one of the greatest deterrents to employment for many reasons, such as pensions and other benefits, which become costly to employers for new employees of advanced age, and the partiality of many large companies to training their own executives.

Other personal data, we think, need not be excluded from your résumé. The employment opportunities for qualified blacks and other ethnic groups are expanding; an equal opportunity employer may be able to utilize information about your race to your advantage. Employment opportunities for qualified women are growing apace. Your height and weight will be of value only in the entertainment field. We prefer that separation or divorce be stated in a résumé, but this is a matter of personal preference.

14. **Hobbies.** Mention interesting hobbies; omit commonplace ones, except golf and tennis, which accomplish wide rapport. Outstanding excellence in any sport or hobby should be mentioned.

15. **Languages.** A knowledge of languages other than English may be mandatory in an international business and important or helpful in many other activities. Include any language proficiency.

16. **Reason for leaving last job.** Some recruiters consider this information to be an important part of a résumé. We prefer its *omission* because the explanation can be cumbersome and disadvantageous. Furthermore, it can normally have no positive influence on gaining an interview. *The reason for leaving your last job is a matter to be discussed at a personal interview when you can explain it at length.* However, almost everyone has had one disastrous job experience. It may even be an advantage—one story, possibly apocryphal, has it that a large employer receiving hundreds of applications for a position decided to exclude all résumés that did not show one job failure!

There are many reasons for leaving a job either by choice or involuntarily. A frequent reason is personality conflict. Whether your fault or your employer's and colleagues', it is to your disadvantage before the prospective employer has had an opportunity to make a personal assessment of you during an interview. A résumé giving "personality conflict" as the reason for leaving a job may become discarded before a personal interview takes place; it is a reason that can give rise to complicated and initially unfavorable psychological reactions.

One highly placed manager was dismissed after 20 years because he had accepted a small gift from an appreciative customer four years earlier. In fact, his dismissal was not for this transgression per se. Some of his subordinates had been accepting large bribes from customers, of which he was unaware, but perhaps should not have been. His earlier acceptance of one small gift placed him in an untenable position, which, management felt, could not remain an exception. There was a bit of post-Watergate morality in this corporate action, and near-tragedy for the employee. Many people will find it difficult to understand why a company's chief executive officer is free to spend millions for bribing foreign government employees to get business or hundreds of thousands for illegal campaign contributions while lesser infractions are heavily penalized. It is a subject needing discussion. Certainly most prospective employers would overlook this type of transgression after the applicant's full explanation during an interview—an explanation difficult or impossible to include in a résumé.

Some reasons for leaving a job are easily explainable, such as mergers and discontinuance of business. These reasons can be given in a résumé.

Several jobs held in a short period of time need to be explained if the period is important to the chronology of the résumé. The period can be omitted entirely if it occurs early in your career, for example.

Employment gaps should be explained or closed as fully as possible. Gaps occurring during a recession will be understood by your prospective employer. For those gaps very difficult to justify you might consult your friends or former employers. Such terms as "consultant" and "freelance worker" are poorly received except in areas where freelancing is common (artists and writers, for example).

17. **Security clearance.** If your past or present employment is security sensitive, specify the level of your security clearance.

18. **Aptitude and psychological tests.** Employers tend to think that most tests other than their own have little validity. In fact, such tests frequently are too generalized or diffused to be of significance. Omit test results from your résumé, unless excerpts of singular appropriateness can be used to show qualifications objectively.

19. **Photographs.** Most of the executives recruiting for business do not consider photographs important. Nevertheless, a résumé impact can

be increased by including a small (2½ by 2½ inches) clearly defined candid snapshot in color (passport-type photographs are usually of poor quality).Remember that photographs with the subject posed for artistic effect are inappropriate in business résumés. Paste the photograph in the upper left or right hand corner of the first résumé page. Photographs are essential in the résumé of an entertainer or model and should be 8 by 10 inches or larger.

20. **Art decoration.**   Simple decoration can improve a résumé. However, because "one man's meat is another man's poison" use art devices with great care.

21. **Graphs and charts.**   Graphs and charts usually add little to a résumé unless of professional quality. A simple curve showing sales increases is not impressive. On the other hand, a 10 year bar chart of sales and profit increases or a curve of dramatic increases in your income can make valid points.

22. **Testimonials.**   Testimonials can serve effectively as objective evaluations, provided that you can present them without appearing to be boastful. Testimonials can be placed in any appropriate part of your résumé, particularly on a summary page or in a summary paragraph, or when discussing your handling of important responsibilities.

23. **Civil service grades.**   In seeking a job with the government or in indicating the governmental level of your responsibilities to a private employer, mention of the civil service grade is useful.

RÉSUMÉ READERS' CRITICISMS

The criticisms listed below are those most commonly expressed by résumé readers. You will observe that many of them are in exact opposition. There is no way to write a résumé that will appeal to every reader. Fit your résumé to the type of individual whom you expect to be reading it.

1. **Too long.**   The résumé is not concise, interesting, and relevant. A person required to read hundreds or thousands of résumés, however, may find any résumé that exceeds one page to be too long. Keep a résumé short if it is aimed at a lower echelon personnel executive or an employment agency.

2. **Too short.**   The résumé does not give the reader an opportunity to make a proper evaluation.

3. **Too condensed.**   Paragraphs and sentences are too closely written for easy reading. It is preferable to expand spatially sentences, paragraphs, and white space rather than to try to get two pages of easy-to-read writing on one page.

4. **Too wordy.** The description is verbose, with several words used for what could have been expressed in one or two.

5. **Too slick.** The résumé is so well prepared as to be inappropriate for the individual presenting it and must therefore have been written by someone else. This evaluation leads the reader to suspect that the subject's qualifications are exaggerated.

6. **Too amateurish.** The applicant cannot express himself, which would be a liability on the job.

7. **Poorly reproduced.** The résumé is carelessly reproduced, especially when duplicated by photocopying.

8. **Misspellings and bad grammar abound.** Spelling and grammatical errors in a résumé show lack of the primary skills necessary for accomplishment. Poor spellers need not be low achievers, but a poor speller who does not compensate for this deficiency by having another person proofread the résumé shows bad judgment. Bad grammar is inexcusable at the executive and professional levels.

9 **Reason for leaving last job omitted.** This has been discussed elsewhere in this book.

10. **Date of availability omitted.** If you apply for a position months ahead of the time when you can start work, include the date of your availability.

11. **Geographical preference omitted.** Any geographical preferences or limitations regarding location of employment should be specified in a résumé.

12. **Objective omitted.** This has been discussed elsewhere.

13. **Poorly expressed.** If you are unable to prepare your own résumé, have someone else write it for you.

14. **Résumé is boastful.** Boastfulness is an unattractive quality. Be realistic about yourself, but do not bluster, overestimate, or exaggerate.

15. **Résumé is dishonest.** You have claimed to have expertise that you do not possess.

16. **Salary information lacking.** This has been discussed elsewhere.

17. **Résumé is "gimmicky."** It contains words, structure, decoration, or material that departs so much from the norm that it is unacceptable.

18. **Sufficient data lacking.** The material is insufficient for a proper evaluation. You may have tried to condense to one page experience that requires several pages for explanation.

SECTION   10

The Right Résumé—
Strong and Positive

Most of the individuals whose résumés appear in this book sound like achievers. In fact, some may have had disappointing careers. Others have accomplished something, but not enough, in the companies for which they worked. They might have succeeded in other companies or under other circumstances. The faults measured by the requirements of one position, or by the definition of one management, can be virtues when measured by different criteria.

Your résumé should make you, too, sound like an achiever. Forget your negative aspects and stress your positive attributes. Self-analysis, aided by suggestions in this book, may reveal talents of which you have been unaware. Your chronological job history may disclose accomplishments you have underestimated. When written down, your accomplishments may sound better than you expected. They may be superior when compared to those of others doing similar jobs.

If your career has been less successful than you had hoped, it need not continue to be so. Your résumé is a means of escape from career disappointment or mediocrity to career fulfillment. It is not dishonest to have your résumé accent your most positive characteristics. No one is perfect. *You* may be just what some employer is looking for. In another position your positive attributes may bring you the degree of success that has eluded you in the past, whatever your present level of accomplishment.

Your résumé is a way to gain an interview. Make it as strong as possible to achieve that end. You cannot help yourself or anyone else with a weak résumé.

ANALYSIS OF RÉSUMÉ USERS: ENTRY POSITION

The average age is 24.5.
Females are 20% of sample.

SECTION 11

The Ten Résumé
Styles

There are about 10 recognized résumé styles or forms, with an infinite number of variations and combinations. The examples given in this book should help you in choosing among them. Our recommendations appear on pages 2 to 3. The 10 styles are discussed in detail in the sections that follow.

1. *Basic Résumé.*
2. *Chronological Résumé.*
3. *Chronological Résumé with Summary Page.*
4. *Functional Résumé.*
5. *Harvard Résumé.*
6. *Functional-by-Company (Institution) Résumé. Company* here refers to an incorporated or unincorporated business. *Institution* is an organization with a social, educational, or religious purpose, such as a school, church, hospital, prison, and foundation.
7. *Creative Résumé.*
8. *Narrative Résumé.*
9. *Professional Résumé.*
10. *Accomplishment Résumé.*

The word *form* is used to mean style of résumé. *Format* refers to the physical aspects of a résumé, such as its margins, headlines, underlining, and page size.

Remember that the accomplishments listed in your résumé need not be notable achievements, but achievements within the level of your responsibility only. Whether you are an office boy, a clerk, a supervisor, a manager, or a president, you can have accomplishments that are significant in relation to your job and job objective.

SECTION 12
Basic Résumé

The *Basic Résumé,* best suited for those entering the job market, should contain the following items (their order may vary).

1. Name, address with zip code, and telephone number with area code.
2. Personal data (age, marital status, health, willingness to travel or relocate, date of availability).
3. Objectives.
4. Education (honors, awards, high class standing).
5. Extracurricular activities.
6. Languages other than English.
7. Summer jobs.
8. Military service.
9. Hobbies (if interesting).

This is a standard form. We recommend that job qualifications be added, if they can be properly expressed, immediately after objectives. Keep this résumé to one page. Use the *Basic Résumé* whenever work experience is very limited. Any important job experience that does exist should be described before education.

Examples of *Basic Résumé* follow.

INFLUENCE OF COLLEGE EDUCATION ON LIFETIME EARNINGS

U.S. Department of Labor statistics consistently show that a college education signifi-cantly increases lifetime earnings. The 1972 data, for example, indicate the following:

Educational level	Lifetime earnings (ages 25–64)	Increase in lifetime earnings
Four years of college	$668,100	70%
One to three years of college	$461,000	18%
High school	$393,000	

In their recent study, *The Declining Value of College Going,* Freeman and Holloman state that "by all relevant measures the economic status of college graduates is deteriorating, with employment prospects for the young declining exceptionally sharply." This assess-ment, and its connotation for the future, is not uniformly shared. According to Herbert Bienstock, head of the Bureau of Labor Statistics in New York, long-term government projections show that the demand for college graduates will grow at three times the rate of demand for all workers in the United States labor force. Furthermore, jobless rates in March 1975 were 3% for college graduates and 15% for high school dropouts.

Stephen B. Withey, author of *A Degree and What Else,* writes in a Carnegie Com-mission on Higher Education report that students going through college increase their interest in esthetic and cultural values and progress on the "social maturity scale" to a much greater extent than do noncollege individuals. They have a greater ability to shape their "material future," greater job security, better career prospect, and greater job satis-faction.

EXAMPLE OF BASIC RÉSUMÉ

23 Redondo Drive   (123) 456-7890
La Jolla, Calif. (zip)

RESUME
of
RICHARD SMITH

PERSONAL DATA: Born 3/10/51, single, excellent health.

OBJECTIVE:

Association with a communications or other company in an entry position with opportunity for general management consistent with ability to contribute.

QUALIFICATIONS:

Good education, consistently high academic grades, willingness to work hard to
establish capability; concerned with and interested in major U. S. and world problems; active in causes; experienced in working with general public during summer
jobs and in retail selling since graduating from college. Volunteer work 1974 to
date. Harmonious, articulate, diligent. Senior year of high school in Thailand.
Rudimentary knowledge of French and German.

EDUCATION:

B. A., Government, University of Pennsylvania, Philadelphia, Pa., 1973.
Courses in Government: U. S., South Africa, Latin America, France.
Courses in: Principles of Management, Economics I and II, International Business,
    Business Ethics, Fundamentals of Public Speaking, Oral Interpretation.
Dean's list, two years.

EXTRA-CURRICULAR ACTIVITIES:

Football, lacrosse, handball; librarian assistant; mail room messenger; R.O.T.C.

BUSINESS EXPERIENCE:

Nov. 22-Dec. 24, 1973   THE MAY COMPANY, Long Beach, Calif.

TOY SALESMAN for branch of leading department store.

SUMMER JOBS:

1969-1973   DEPT. of PARKS and RECREATION, La Jolla, Calif.

June to Nov. 1973, GATE ATTENDANT, beach area; June to Sept. 1972, POOL
GATEMAN; June to Sept. 1971, LOCKER ROOM ATTENDANT; June to Sept. 1970,
LOCKER ROOM ATTENDANT; June to Sept. 1969, PARK ATTENDANT. Collected
revenues, checked residency, painted, cleaned beach.

HOBBIES: Numismatics, philately, chess.

REFERENCES AND FURTHER DATA ON REQUEST

DISCUSSION

Basic Résumé. The Smith résumé arouses interest at once. Here is a young man who knows the general area in which he would like to work and without boastfulness expresses the qualifications he knows he possesses. Probably only a few students could be selected for study in Thailand. He attained academic honors in college. He worked during the summer vacation months. His extracurricular activities were broad. His hobbies are intellectual. His studies were chosen with a business career in mind.

The résumé is patterned for easy readability and logical sequence with education taking precedence over business experience because of its greater importance at this career stage.

If the employment had included important learning experience relevant to job objective it might have preceded education.

EXAMPLE OF BASIC RÉSUMÉ

AARON SCHWARTZ

12 44th Street
Bellmore, N. Y. 11375
(123) 456-7890

RESUME

PERSONAL DATA: Age 23, single, excellent health. Interested in Classical Music, Archaeology, Architecture, City Planning. Travel in Europe and Israel.

OBJECTIVE: Trainee in International Division of a Corporation in Banking, Sales or Public Relations in the United States, Europe, or Africa; with opportunity to advance to management.

QUALIFICATIONS: Studies in International Economics and International Law. Intensive study in the history, sociology, political and economic development of Africa, inter-African relations, international relations of African states, U. S., African foreign policy.

EDUCATION:

1972   B. A.   University of Maryland – 3 years
Baltimore, Maryland

M. A.   New York University, School of Advanced International Studies, New York, N. Y. – 2 years

Awarded Fellowship and full tuition for fourth and fifth years of study.

1970   Ecole Universitaire Des Hautes Etudes Europeenes, Geneva, Switzerland

Awarded Fellowship for summer study of International Organization and French.

LANGUAGES: Fluent French, good reading comprehension of German and Hebrew.

EXTRA-CURRICULAR
ACTIVITIES:

1970-1972   Tutoring at University

Summer 1969   First National City Bank, Teller

Summers
1967-1968   Hotel Plaza, New York City
Accounting Auditor for inventory and cost control.

REFERENCES AND FURTHER DATA ON REQUEST

DISCUSSION

Basic Résumé. The Schwartz résumé utilizes a different physical style from the preceding résumé, with the résumé elements headlined in the left hand margin and the data indented. The choice of style is one of aesthetics, though it also conserves space.

The first paragraph shows at once a young man with wide interests. His objective is quite definite and his educational preparation for it has been well planned.

A high level of intelligence is indicated by the fellowship awards. Knowledge of languages is important to the objective, and proficiency was attained in languages of major importance.

Summers were not wasted.

The subject recognized the increasing influence of the emerging nations and planned his studies accordingly.

The résumé is one that should engage the immediate interest of employers recruiting promising future executives.

EXAMPLE OF BASIC RÉSUMÉ

SAMUEL STOUT   237 Richelieu Ave.
                                                         Bronx, N. Y. 11210
                                                         (123) 445-6789
                              RESUME

PERSONAL DATA:

   Age 22, single, healthy. Extensively travelled in United States, Europe,
   British Isles, Canada. Speak and understand some French.

OBJECTIVE:

   Position in Financial Department of Corporation, Institution.

EDUCATION:

   1971   B. S., Pace University, School of Commerce, New York, N. Y.
           Major, Banking and Finance: Corporate Finance, Management,
           Investment Analysis, Money Markets, Economics, Accounting.

           Admitted to Phi Alpha Kappa, Honor Finance Society, for attain-
           ing 3.5 index. Cumulative 4 year index: 3.3 of possible 4.0.

           Member of Finance Society, Pre-Law Society.

   1971-
   Present Attending New York Law School (night classes).

EXPERIENCE:

   May 1-Dec. 30, 1972   Land Development Corp.

           As ASSISTANT TO THE PRESIDENT, gained practical financial ex-
           perience in helping to rescue near bankrupt corporation. Involved
           in decision-making and negotiations.

           Met and negotiated with substantial investors from all over the
           world in connection with Company plans for an underwriting.

           Participated in surveys and studies of land development project
           in Arizona.

           Also learned about water desalinization.

   Experience in Security Brokerage through part-time work in Uncle's business.

MILITARY SERVICE: 1968   U. S. NAVAL RESERVE, Boatswains Mate 3/C.

                 REFERENCES AND FURTHER DATA ON REQUEST

DISCUSSION

Basic Résumé. The Stout résumé utilizes the same form as the Schwartz résumé, with a slightly narrower indentation accommodating almost the identical number of words. Again, the form is a matter of choice. The fact that one has traveled extensively is usually well worth including in a résumé because travel is educational and contributes to self-development.

This young man's educational experience was outstanding and easily takes precedence over his business experience even though that was unique and interesting.

Although a legal education is not directly related to finance, it is nevertheless excellent training for any business career and, added to undergraduate studies in finance, will create an individual of substantial educational background that can be later utilized for professional management progress.

This résumé should be well received by executive recruiters.

EXAMPLE OF BASIC RÉSUMÉ

1 East 96th Street   (123) 456-7890
New York, N. Y. 10022

RESUME
of
THOMAS MUFFINS

OBJECTIVE: Entry level position in corporate finance or in financial in-
                    stitution in investment, portfolio management, trust depart-
                    ment; or in marketing; or in any position offering challenge
                    and opportunity.

QUALIFICATIONS: Analytical, motivated, meet and work well with people at
                    all levels. Willing to work hard to achieve goals, good in
                    oral and written communications, imaginative.

PERSONAL DATA: Age 22, single; willing to relocate.

EDUCATION: B. A., Lafayette College, Easton, Pa., 1973.

EXTRA-CURRICULAR   Chess, Government and History Clubs. Varsity Cross
ACTIVITIES: Country, Manager, Cross Country and Track, Intramural
                    Basketball and Squash.

LANGUAGES: Write and speak Spanish (semi-fluent).

MEMBERSHIPS: Y.M.C.A.

HOBBIES: Chess, investments, squash, stamp collecting, travel
                    (travelled extensively throughout Europe).

SUMMER   ASSISTANT PARK RANGER, Sir Walter Scott National Park,
EMPLOYMENT: near Edinburgh, Scotland, 1970.

                    ADMINISTRATIVE assignment with Liedersdorf & Co.,
                    Richmond, Va., 1969.

EXPERIENCE: July 1973-Feb. 1974, NATIONAL INSURANCE CO., New York,
                    N. Y.

                    MANAGEMENT TRAINEE for $5.0 billion property and casualty
                    insurance company with objective of career in production.
                    Received on-the-job training in all departments; wrote review
                    and analysis of selected area of operations of each depart-
                    ment. Assigned to administrative management position; de-
                    cided that opportunities did not coincide with objectives.

REFERENCES AND FURTHER DATA ON REQUEST

DISCUSSION

Basic Résumé.   Mr. Muffins states his objective clearly and leaves room for acceptance of any entry position offering opportunity. He lists qualifications that would be attractive to any employer without sounding brash or egotistical. Summer employment was both interesting and, in one instance, related to objective. The business experience indicates that his employer recognized his abilities by providing broad training for him. But this young man was not satisfied with his assignment and, rather than waste time, submitted his resignation to look for a new position.

Hobbies and extracurricular activities denote wide interests and originality.

The total impact of the résumé is that this 22 year old man has used time to accomplish a great deal, and the promise of future success is implicit in this brief sketch.

S E C T I O N   13
Chronological Résumé

The *Chronological Résumé* is the one most frequently used by applicants who have job experience. The form offers the writer the best opportunity to "highlight" achievements and the reader the best opportunity to gauge the applicant's qualifications. The work experience is shown in reverse chronological order, the last or present job being given first. The various positions held at one company should also be described in reverse chronological order. This order shows the applicant's growth and development—characteristics of great interest to employers. The elements of the *Chronological Résumé* are as follows:

1. Name, address, and telephone number.
2. Objective.
3. Name of the company of most recent or present employment.

   - Brief description of the company.
   - Responsibilities.
   - Accomplishments (treat each level of assignment as if it were a different employer).

4. Name of the company of next most recent employment.

   - Brief description of the company.
   - Responsibilities.
   - Accomplishments.

   Continue as above for each relevant employment, going back to your first job. If earlier employment is unrelated to your present objective, summarize it briefly in a catchall sentence or paragraph. Omit mention of inappropriate or undignified jobs—jobs that are unrelated to the one being sought, or jobs that poorly reflect your qualities.
5. Military service (delete this heading if inappropriate).
6. Education.
7. Extracurricular activities (including summer jobs).
8. Accreditations (C.P.A., C.L.U., Real Estate Broker, Licensed Engineer, and so forth).
9. Professional memberships.
10. Community activities.
11. Hobbies.
12. Personal data.

The *Chronological Résumé* may be two or more pages in length. Remember the rules: conciseness, relevance, and interest.

Examples of *Chronological Résumé* follow (p. 37).

JOB COMPETITION

Here is a typical response to an attractive advertisement for a senior marketing executive in a Tuesday edition of *The Wall Street Journal*.

Number of answers	310
In the New York area	186
Outside the New York area	124
Résumés received	294
Letters received	16
Applicants who are employed	257
Applicants who are unemployed	19
Not clear whether employed or unemployed	34
Salary stated	198
Salary not stated	112
Undergraduate degree	180
Master's degree	80
Doctoral degree	7
No degree	43

SMALL AND LARGE COMPANIES AS JOB SOURCES

Fast-growing smaller companies are among the best targets for employment; they have no reservoir of staff and *must* hire at all levels from outside. Many large corporations prefer to promote from within if possible. They are very important employers at entry levels. This does not mean they are not a target of an employment search at any level; it means only that fast-growing companies should be sought out in addition to the very large companies.

EXAMPLE OF CHRONOLOGICAL RÉSUMÉ

1776 Patriot St.   (123) 456-7890
Boston, Mass. (zip.)

RESUME

of

MARY MIDDLETON

Employment Objective in the Following Areas:

INVESTMENT BANKING   -   Municipal financial consulting; new issues; new business; private placements; financial services; institu-
tional sales; research.

COMMERCIAL BANKING -   Urban affairs, money market, municipal lending,
financial services.

Education includes:

M.B.A., B.S., superior grades, 3.7 on the 4.0 scale. Finance major.

Personal data:

Age 32, divorced, excellent health; interested in financial analysis, riding,
sports, travel, writing.

Record of Experience:

1968-Present   KUHN MARX & CO., 5 Hancock St., Boston, Mass.

ANALYST, Institutional Department for investment banking company and full-
service retail and institutional brokerage. This department over the past
$5\frac{1}{2}$ years handled approximately 35 new capital projects per year for municipalities in Connecticut involving general obligation or revenue bonds of
about $200 million.

Responsible for:

- preparation and dissemination of information to facilitate new issue financ-
ings by serving as intermediary between municipality and investor.

- assistance to debt issuer to obtain best credit rating possible together
with lowest interest cost.

- creating environment to provide maximum marketability of bonds.

- preparation and finalization of all Official Statements including organization of all pertinent economic and financial data needed for evaluation.

MARY MIDDLETON   PAGE 2

The above responsibilities entailed:

- participation in all preliminary financial discussions with architects, bond
  counsels, house counsel, municipalities, solicitors, trustee banks and/or
  paying agents, syndicate members, issuers, investors and major banks and
  insurance companies, financial firms and salesmen.

- risk analysis, financing concepts and closing sales. Personally responsible
  for many salesmen's orders up to $2.6 million.

- examination of feasibility of capital proposals, reviewing feasibility reports
  prepared by consultants and major accounting firms, suggesting modifications as necessary to assure successful underwriting, inclusion of security
  provisions, rate covenants, earnings tests, reserve capitalization, analysis
  of financial statements including balance sheets, break-even points and re-
  checking to assure validity of risk/equity relationships.

- contacts with regulatory agencies at State and Federal levels.

The carrying out of these various responsibilities resulted in:

- saving issuers thousands of dollars in basis points by achieving higher ratings from rating services through personal presentations, i. e., upgrading
  ratings, holding marginal ratings, reversing lower ratings, sometimes getting
  a higher rating from one service than another and thereby mitigating the
  lower rating.

- ability to underwrite issues in difficult markets.

- specifically, for example, causing both Moody and Standard & Poor's to upgrade one $15.9 million Refunding School Authority Issue in 1973 which other-
  wise might have produced an underwriting loss.

- reduction of underwriting and other market risks.

- protection of firm against civil or criminal suits for non-disclosure with con-
  comitant result of full profit.

- repeat business for the firm.

<u>1964-1968</u>   DUN AND STANDARD CORP., 27 Wall Street, N. Y., N. Y.

Member of EDITORIAL STAFF, WRITER AND ANALYST of and for "Bond Outlook"
for publisher of financial data on securities with well-known investment advisory service to clients.

- prepared weekly analysis of new bond issues.

- reviewed and evaluated municipal credit.

MARY MIDDLETON   PAGE 3

- analyzed economic, social, political and geographical data.

- reported on city and state general obligation, revenue and construction bonds.

- studied and evaluated annual municipal financial statements, audits, budgets, capital improvement programs.

- evaluated debt structures, histories and trends.

- reviewed and weighed qualitative factors of administration, organization, structure, efficiency and growth factors.

- utilized all types of financial data, Federal Reserve and Census Bureau publications.

Accustomed to personal interview and liaison activities with municipal officials, business managers, financial advisors and consultants and bank executives. Experience additionally included:

- training analysts.

- analysis of Standard & Poor's ratings on 8,000 issues.

- development of advertising themes.

- providing data and story-lines for financial writers.

- diversified special reports, summaries and analysis.

1961-1964   WACHOVIA TRUST CO., New York, N. Y.

RESEARCH ASSISTANT after starting as Statistical Clerk for one of largest banks in the U. S.

- worked directly with Senior Municipal Analyst and Senior Vice President.

- prepared analytical reports on municipal securities for Officers Investment Committee and Board of Directors.

- provided reports forming a basis for portfolio decisions.

- provided complete supporting statistical data and analyses.

- utilized all sources of financial and economic data as appropriate.

- maintained financial and economic charts.

REFERENCES AND FURTHER DATA ON REQUEST

DISCUSSION

Chronological Résumé. The Middleton résumé is very comprehensive and could have been written in several other forms, such as a *Functional Résumé* or *Chronological with Summary Page Résumé*. The chronological form was chosen because the sequence of experience shows continuous growth.

The summary page was omitted in this instance to keep the résumé short; no summary is really needed to explain the obvious high qualifications of the subject.

The résumé is written in the language of a professional expressing knowledge of her subject with literacy and compactness. Her work is specialized and complicated. Any reader will know at once that here is a highly capable individual. Despite the résumé's comprehensiveness there is still much that remains to be explored in a personal interview.

Age, education, and personal data are clearly and briefly expressed at the outset because most are highly favorable and need no extended comment.

ANALYSIS OF RÉSUMÉ USERS: FINANCE

Chief financial officer, treasurer, controller, accounting, brokerage, financial research, and intermediate positions.

The salary range is $7000 to $80,000.

The median is $19,000.

In percentages:

   45% earn from $18,000 to $26,000.
   25% earn from $12,000 to $18,000.
   10% earn over $26,000.
   20% earn from $7000 to $10,000.

The age range is 24 to 61.

The average age is 38.3.

Some 50% are in their 30s.

Females are 2.5% of the total.

Chronological Résumé
with Summary Page

The *Chronological Résumé with Summary Page* is the most effective form of résumé for middle to upper business management as well as in some other vocations. The summary page interprets the résumé and quickly provides the gist of the applicant's case. Remember that the summary page is always the *first* page of the résumé. It is written *last,* however, because it is based on the material appearing in the chronological part of the résumé, which must be written *first.*

A summary page establishes rapport and interest and creates the curiosity to learn more about the applicant's background in the subsequent pages. Psychologically it compliments the reader by recognizing that his or her time is valuable and by providing the opportunity to make a quick appraisal.

The summary page can also be used to "beef up" a basically weak résumé.

The summary page, however, is an extra page. If you are concerned about the length of your résumé, eliminate the summary page or reduce its content to a brief paragraph or two to be placed at the beginning of the résumé. You will find examples of résumés with full summary pages and with reduced summaries.

Because *Chronological Résumé with Summary Page* is difficult to prepare, it is explained in detail in the pages that follow. In our annotated example page 2 appears first because the summary page, page 1, is *written last.*

EXAMPLE OF CHRONOLOGICAL RÉSUMÉ
WITH SUMMARY PAGE

375 Broadalban Road   (177) 377-4777
Ephrata, N. C. 43215

RESUME

of

DUNCAN SMITH

Qualified As

SENIOR MANAGEMENT EXECUTIVE

* * *   Record of consistent profit contributions amounting to
         millions of dollars in general management, marketing,
         production in the U. S., Canada and internationally;
         accustomed for the last ten years to autonomous multi-
         division P. & L. responsibility and responsible for at
         least eight turn-around situations involving significant
         figures.

* * *   Equipped to use latest management sciences including
         PERT, CPM and other network techniques to accomplish
         Company goals.

* * *   Intimately familiar with the metal-working industry and
         with sophisticated machinery and equipment in a broad
         area of manufacturing.

* * *   Characterized by others as an inspiring leader, incisive
         in identifying problems, imaginative in finding and im-
         plementing solutions, strong in comprehensive, accurate
         planning to improve profitability.

FOR FURTHER DATA PLEASE SEE FOLLOWING PAGES

DUNCAN SMITH

BUSINESS EXPERIENCE:

1970-Present   LEAF MACHINERY DIVISION, BRF, INC.
                             Winston-Salem, N. C.

VICE PRESIDENT, GENERAL MANAGER of $45 million tobacco machinery manu-
facturing division of $700 million leisure products conglomerate. Reported to
parent corporate Group Vice President. Supervised V. P., R. & D., Controller, Director of Marketing, European and South American Directors.

Responsibility:

- P. & L. for U. S. division and plants in France, U. K., Brazil, and marketing headquarters in Switzerland.

Achievements:

- U. K. Division lost $250,000 first quarter 1970; by August Division was op-
  erating profitably with earnings of $80,000.
- Reduced inflated U. S. payroll by $235,000.
- Successfully introduced three new products of complex technology.
- Increased Division revenue 21% and pre-tax profits 13%.
- Improved return on assets from 13.8% to 14.6%.
- Prepared, submitted and implemented five-year plan yielding compounded an-
  nual growth in pre-tax profits of 13.3%.

These accomplishments were engineered by the use of PERT, Critical Path
Method and other network techniques to improve production, eliminate bottlenecks; by repricing; by implementing plans which had been made but not acted
upon; and by creating a new sales program.

1967-1970   THOMAS & SESSIONS, Springfield, Mo.

1969-1970   ASSISTANT to the PRESIDENT of $80 million manufacturer
of meters, electric sub-assemblies, fractional horsepower motors and other products.

1967-1969   PRESIDENT of autonomous Canadian Division with sales
of $15 million. Responsible for:

- Management of complete staff: finance, sales, manufacturing.
- Divisional profit and loss.
- Assisting the President of parent company.
- Presiding at Directors' and Stockholders' meetings.

Accomplishments:

- In 1967 losses were above $$\frac{1}{2}$$ million annually; by end 1969 losses were
  eliminated and profits stood at all-time high of $1.137 million.

DUNCAN SMITH   PAGE 3

This was accomplished by consolidating motor operations, reducing overhead, eliminating ineffective department in production area, re-aligning production facilities, changing sales plans and reassigning sales responsibilities.

1962-1967   W. H. THOMPSON & CO., Harrisburg, Pa.

This Company manufacturers castings, wire, rod and strip, electrical wire and cable, fractional horsepower motors and other industrial products. Volume of $300 million.

1964-1967   VICE PRESIDENT, INTERNATIONAL OPERATIONS. Reported to President. Supervised Director of International Marketing and Managers in Canada, Mexico, Brazil, U. K., Europe, Australia. Responsible for:

- Profit and Loss for 17 international plants, and all exports.

Accomplishments:

- Increased pre-tax profits from $1.07 million to $1.69 million including complete amortization of start-up costs in five new plants.
- Increased volume of manufactured product from $40 million to $45.5 million.
- Restored profitability to Canadian plant operating at a loss of $52,000.
- Achieved turn-around in SARE Division from loss of $350,000 to profit of $120,000; similarly in Netherlands and Brazilian companies.

1962-1964   VICE PRESIDENT, W. H. Thompson & Co. of Canada, Toronto, Ontario.
Supervised General Sales Manager, Controller and three Plant Managers. Responsible for:

- Profit and Loss for three manufacturing locations and six product lines in $12 million division.

Achievements included:

- Improvement in pre-tax profit from $396,000 to $578,000.
- Increased revenue from $13.0 million to $15.1 million.
- Reversed severe loss trend at Canadian wire plant to profit over a period of three years rising from $127,000 to $374,000.
- Improved operation at Rubberoid Plant from loss of $50,000 to a profit of $400,000.

1953-1962   VANADIUM METAL WIRE WORKS, Alloy Division, E. H. Humbolt & Co., Pittsburgh, Pa.

GENERAL MANAGER with supporting staff of Assistant Works Manager,

DUNCAN SMITH   PAGE 4

Plant Superintendent, Accountant, Metallurgist, Production and Quality Control Managers and Chief Industrial Engineer.

- started as District Sales Manager and progressed successively to Regional Sales Manager, Assistant General Sales Manager, Sales Manager.

Accomplishments:

- in first year of responsibility as General Manager turned loss of $20/ 30,000 per month to annual profit of $300,000 with subsequent increase to $600,000.

Offered and accepted position with Vanadium (as described).

MILITARY SERVICE:

1941-1943   UNITED STATES AIR FORCE, Captain

EDUCATION:

B. S., Engineering, 1949, University of Pittsburgh, Pittsburgh, Pa.

Graduate work in Business Management at Northwestern and Michigan State.

COMMUNITY ACTIVITIES:

Chairman, Board of Directors, National Hospital, Winston-Salem, N. C.

Chairman, Community Chest, Winston-Salem, N. C.

Member, National Presidential Committee to Study Government Options.

HONORS:

Winston-Salem Citizen-of-the-Year Award.

HOBBIES:

Tennis, golf, shooting (National 12 Bore Champion).

PERSONAL DATA:

Born 3/31/28, married, two children, excellent health, willing to relocate.

REFERENCES AND FURTHER DATA ON REQUEST

ANALYSIS OF RÉSUMÉ USERS: GENERAL EXECUTIVES

Vice-presidents, general managers, chief executive officers, and individuals who provide no clue to their specialization.

The salary range is $14,500 to $200,000.
The median salary is $33,600.
The age range is 28 to 62.
The average age is 43.3.
There are no females in the sample.
Age in percentages

28% are in their 30s.
33% are in their 40s.
28% are in their 50s.

DISCUSSION

Chronological Résumé with Summary Page. The Duncan Smith résumé is a good example of a true executive résumé, as opposed to a run-of-the-mill résumé. It is longer than most because the subject has a long history of accomplishments. The form of résumé was selected because there is nothing to hide in his chronology, with achievements increasing in each successive position. The résumé provides a strong basis for selection for an interview and for an interesting interview discussion. A résumé of this kind could be written only by a man who is supremely confident that there is no area of management in which he does not have experience and knowledge and that he can support all his claims.

This man creates a favorable attitude even before an interview. If his interview techniques and his actual experience as brought out in an interview are as good as his writing, he is assured of employment.

The summary page is used in this instance to express the highlights of his career and offer some material contributing to his total image. It should make the reader want to read the résumé itself.

The following pages show how this résumé was developed.

THE PRECEDING CHRONOLOGICAL RÉSUMÉ WITH SUMMARY
PAGE ANNOTATED TO SHOW HOW IT WAS WRITTEN

DUNCAN SMITH   Page 2

BUSINESS EXPERIENCE:

<u>Page 1 is written last</u>.

1970-Present   LEAF MACHINERY DIVISION,
                BRF, INC., Winston-Salem,
                N.C.

Period of employment and name of
company.

VICE PRESIDENT, GENERAL MANAGER OF
$45 million tobacco machinery manufac-
turing division of $700 million leisure
products conglomerate. Reported to
parent corporate Group Vice President.
Supervised V.P., R. & D., Controller
Director of Marketing, European and
South American Directors.

Title.
Description of kind and size of
company; reporting relationship;
supervisory relationships.
Evaluation of a candidate is improved when one knows in what
areas he or she worked.

Responsibility:

- P. & L. responsibility for U.S.
  division and plants in France, U.K.,
  Brazil, and marketing headquarters in
  Switzerland.

Nature of responsibilities.

Achievements:

- U.K. Division lost $250,000 first
  quarter 1970; by August Division was
  operating profitably with earnings of
  $80,000, a swing of more than $$\frac{1}{2}$$
  million.

Turnaround no. 1.

- Reduced inflated U.S. payroll by
  $250,000.

Got rid of non-productive employees.

- Successfully introduced three new
  products of complex technology.

Managed <u>production, marketing,
finance</u>.

- Increased Division revenue 21% and
  pre-tax profits 13%.

Contributed profit increase.

- Improved return on assets from 13.8%
  to 14.6%.

Measured company progress in terms
of <u>financial</u> executive.

- Prepared, submitted and implemented
  five-year plan yielding compounded
  annual growth in pre-tax profits of
  13.3%.

Made plans and carried them out.

These accomplishments were engineered
by the use of PERT, Critical Path Method
and other net-work techniques to improve
production, eliminate bottlenecks; by repricing; by implementing plans which had

Although this man does not have a
graduate degree, the tools he used
show a continuing study of management techniques. Potential employees
can gauge an applicant better if a

DUNCAN SMITH   Page 3

been made but not acted upon; and by creating a new sales program.

1967-1970   THOMAS & SESSIONS
                   Springfield, Mo.

1969-1970, ASSISTANT to the PRESIDENT of $80 million manufacturer of meters, electric sub-assemblies, fractional horsepower motors and other products.

1967-1969, PRESIDENT of autonomous Canadian Division with sales of $15 million. Responsible for:

- Management of complete staff: finance, sales, manufacturing.
- Divisional profit and loss.
- Assisting the President of parent company.
- Presiding at Director's and Stockholders' meetings.

Accomplishments:

- In 1967 losses were above $$\frac{1}{2}$$ million annually; by end 1969 losses were eliminated and profits stood at all-time high of $1.137 million.

This was accomplished by consolidating motor operations, reducing overhead, eliminating ineffective department in production area, re-aligning production facilities, changing sales plans and reassigning sales responsibilities.

1953-1967   W. H. THOMPSON & CO.
                   Harrisburg, Pa.

This company manufactures castings, wire, rod and strip, electrical wire and cable, fractional horsepower motors and other industrial products. Volume $300 million.

1964-1967, VICE PRESIDENT, INTERNATIONAL OPERATIONS. Reported to President.

Supervised Director of International Marketing and Managers in Canada, Mexico, Brazil,

brief description of the methods used to gain the results described is provided.

The same sequence and method are used for each separate employment.

Administered Chief Executive Officer responsibilities.

Turnaround no. 2.

Methods used in accomplishing.

Description of what Company made and its volume.

DUNCAN SMITH   Page 4

U.K., Europe, Australia. Responsible for:

- Profit and loss responsibility for 17   Multi-division responsibility.
  international plants and all exports.

Accomplishments:

- Increased pre-tax profits from $1.07 million   Increased profits.
  to $1.69 million, including complete amorti-
  zation of start-up costs in five new plants.
- Increase volume of manufactured product   Improved production.
  from $40 million to $45.5 million.
- Restored profitability to Canadian plant   Turnaround no. 3.
  operating at a loss of $52,000.
- Achieved turn-around in SARE Division   Turnaround no. 4.
  from loss of $350,000 to profit of
  $120,000; similarly for Netherlands and   Turnaround no. 5.
  Brazilian companies.

1962-1964, VICE PRESIDENT, W. H. Thompson
& Co. of Canada, Toronto, Ontario. Supervised General Sales Manager, Controller, and
three plant managers. Responsible for:

- Profit and loss for three manufacturing
  locations and six product lines in $12
  million division.

Achievements included:

- Improvement in pre-tax profit from   Increased profits.
  $396,000 to $578,000.
- Increased revenue from $13.0 million to   Increased sales.
  $15.0 million.
- Reversed severe loss trend at American   Turnaround no. 6.
  wire plant to profit over a period of three
  years rising from $127,000 to $374,000.
- Improved operation at Rubberoid Plant from   Turnaround no. 7.
  loss of $50,000 to a profit of $400,000.

1953-1962   VANADIUM METAL WIRE WORKS,
                  ALLOY DIVISION, E. H. HUMBOLT
                  & CO., Pittsburgh, Pa.

DUNCAN SMITH   Page 5

GENERAL MANAGER with supporting staff of
Assistant Works Manager, Plant Superintendent, Accountant, Metallurgist, Production
and Quality Control Managers and Chief Industrial Engineer.

- started as District Sales Manager and   Sales experience.
  progressed successively to Regional Sales
  Manager, Assistant General Sales Manager, Sales Manager.

Accomplishments:

- in first year of responsibility as General   Turnaround no. 8.
  Manager turned loss of $20/30,000 per
  month to profit of $300,000 annually with
  subsequent increase to $600,000.

Offered and accepted position with Vanadium
(as described).

MILITARY SERVICE:

1941-1943   UNITED STATES AIR FORCE

CAPTAIN

EDUCATION:

B. S., Engineering, 1949, University of
Pittsburgh, Pittsburgh, Pa.

Graduate work in Business Management at
Northwestern and University of Michigan.

COMMUNITY ACTIVITIES:

Chairman, Board of Directors, National Hos-   Took leading role in community
pital, Winston-Salem, N. C.   activities adding to image of cor-
                                                poration among employees and
Chairman, Community Chest, Winston-   others.
Salem, N. C.

Member, National Presidential Committee to
Study Government Options.

DUNCAN SMITH   Page 6

HONORS:

Winston-Salem Citizen-of-the-Year Award.   Recognized for community activities.

HOBBIES:

Tennis, golf, shooting (National 12 Bore   The hobbies are interesting and well
Champion).   worth including.

PERSONAL DATA:

Born 3/31/28, married, two children,   REFERENCES and FURTHER
excellent health, willing to relocate.   DATA on REQUEST

address   telephone

RESUME

of

DUNCAN SMITH

qualified as

SENIOR MANAGEMENT EXECUTIVE

THIS IS WRITTEN <u>LAST</u> BUT WHEN COMPLETED BECOMES PAGE ONE OF THE RESUME.

*** Record of consistent profit con-
    tributions amounting to millions
    of dollars in general management,
    marketing, production in the U.S,
    Canada and internationally; ac-
    customed for the last ten years
    to autonomous multi-division
    P. & L. responsibility and re-
    sponsibile for at least eight turn-
    around situations involving sig-
    nificant figures.

This is a concise statement of the accomplishments described in the body of the resume and of the nature of this man's responsibilities which were at the highest level (P. & L.) and covering the major divisions of a business: marketing, production, finance.

*** Equipped to use latest manage-
    ment sciences including PERT,
    CPM and other network techniques
    to accomplish company goals.

This is evidence of professional management.

*** Intimately familiar with the metal-
    working industry and with sophis-
    ticated machinery and equipment
    in a broad area of manufacturing.

This statement identified the general area in which management has been exercised.

*** Characterized by others as an in-
    spiring leader, incisive in identi-
    fying problems, imaginative in
    finding and implementing solutions,
    strong in comprehensive, accurate
    planning leading to improved prof-
    itability.

An <u>objective</u> evaluation of the subjects most important qualities.

EXAMPLE OF CHRONOLOGICAL RÉSUMÉ
WITH SUMMARY PAGE WITH VARIATION

275 West 50th Street   Home (212) 321-7654
New York, N. Y. 10012   Office (212) 456-0987

R E S U M E

of

VINCENT BENET

an experienced

EXECUTIVE SALESMAN

* * *   Approximately 15 years of experience with leading company in personal sales, marketing and regional sales
management.

* * *   Record of success in achieving national recognition for
type, quality and volume of sales produced; received
bonuses and awards; more important - produced outstanding profits!

* * *   Experienced in hiring and training salesmen, developing
quotas and objectives, formulating and implementing marketing and sales strategies and techniques.

* * *   A record as hard-working winner with a reputation of being the man "least wanted to be in competition with."

* * *   Enjoy excellent contacts among key personnel of major
companies. Adept at establishing and maintaining productive relationships and experience in customer/public
relations; an exceptional and exciting platform public
speaker.

* * *   37 years old. Bachelor of Arts Degree with honors and
considerable graduate work in Psychology.

* * *   In short, achieved all quotas seven times out of ten
years; in three of these years, quotas had been raised
out of all proportion to previous historical sales - increased sales by 400% - boosted profits.

FOR FURTHER DATA PLEASE SEE FOLLOWING PAGES

VINCENT BENET   Page 2

* Record of success in achieving a 400% increase in sales as a result of effective sales management:

1968-Present   ABC CORP., Freeport, N.Y.

This is a major producer of business machines and data processing equipment.

As SALES MANAGER, Office Products Sales and Data Entry Sales, in the Brooklyn and Queens area, have been responsible for:

- Supervision and training of six salesmen.
- Development of schedules, strategies and techniques to develop leads and increase sales. Brooklyn and Queens are unique in that they have relatively few very large customers. It was, therefore, necessary to tap the potential smaller market. This was done and the region generated 10% of nationwide sales.
- Achieved heavy personal sales and won sales bonuses year after year; became one of the highest producers in the company.
- Participated in the establishment of sales quotas and product mix and developed promotional programs.
- Systematically and effectively converted "low grade sales" to become high grade sales involving increased profitabilities.
- Instituted a regional policy to require cash deposits on orders and substantially decreased cancellations. So dramatic were the results that this became standard company policy.
- Maintained a "get tough" collection policy without sacrifice of good will or cordial public relations.

* Other experience in maximizing sales through modern sales management techniques:

1960-1968   ABC CORP., Boston, Mass.

As SALES MANAGER, supervised a group of salesmen and achieved sales quotas seven out of eight years.

- Maintained continuing market surveys to determine customer needs.
- Worked closely with key personnel of customers and potential customers to maintain sales of accessories and supplies, upgrade equipment and provide corporate technical and maintenance services.
- Nearly tripled personal earnings.
- Designed retail accounting equipment that ultimately resulted in multi-million dollar sales.

* Demonstrated talent for industrial and consumer sales; achieved countrywide leadership:

VINCENT BENET   Page 3

<u>1958-1960</u>   IBM CORP., New York, N.Y.

As ACCOUNT MANAGER/SALES REPRESENTATIVE achieved sales quota each year and was responsible for:

- Development of an outstanding sales record; substantially contributed to my division's becoming the leader on a countrywide performance record.
- Successfully penetrated accounts such as Railway Express, Texaco, American Can and others.

<u>1955</u>   GROLIERE CORPORATION

Sold encyclopaedia door-to-door throughout New York, New Jersey, Massachusetts, Connecticut, Rhode Island, Vermont, etc.   (part-time while attending college)

Finished seventh out of 1000 sales people in a national 20-week contest.

* <u>Military Service</u>:

<u>1953-1955</u>   UNITED STATES NAVY

Served as Instructor at the U.S. Naval Academy at Annapolis. Received special commendation for class' overall proficiency, then the highest in Academy history.

* <u>Education</u>:

<u>1958</u>   UNIVERSITY OF GEORGIA

Received a Bachelor of Arts degree and attained the Dean's List in the senior year.

<u>1969-1974</u>   NEW SCHOOL FOR SOCIAL RESEARCH

Completed several courses in Psychology which contributed to my understanding of human relations and markedly influenced the success of sales activities.

At college, played varsity football, lacrosse, was Sports Editor, worked summers during college.

* <u>Personal Data</u>:

37 years old, married, one child, excellent health.

REFERENCES AND FURTHER DATA ON REQUEST

DISCUSSION

Chronological Résumé with Summary Page with Variation. The variations from norm in the Benet résumé are a final paragraph summarizing his most important assets and headlines emphasizing the outstanding factor in each chronologically listed position. Either variation or both can be used. Headlines can serve to unify the items in a résumé if they are informative, relevant, and important.

This résumé reflects the personality of the subject in the use of punctuation, quoted phrases, and relatively informal language imbued with a sense of excitement.

The summary page serves an effective purpose in giving a special dimension to the subject apart from the material in the résumé.

This is a salesman who sounds like a salesman and would undoubtedly receive invitations for interviews upon submitting this résumé.

A summary page can often be used to incorporate material that does not fit gracefully into the body of a résumé.

S E C T I O N 15
Functional Résumé

The *Functional Résumé* organizes work experience by function, such as general marketing, management, production, finance, or their subfunctions. Chronology is disregarded. To facilitate comparison, we have refashioned one of our *Chronological Résumé* examples into functional form.

The *Functional Résumé* stresses the scope of experience, much as does a summary page. It has the disadvantage of not relating accomplishments to the pertinent company or companies. Most employers are familiar with other companies, especially in the same industry, and take company affiliations into account when judging accomplishments. The same experience is more impressive if gained at a widely known company than at an unknown company.

The writer of a *Functional Résumé,* not being hampered by chronology, can easily change emphasis or camouflage past experience. This is advantageous in cases in which past job experience is best explained in a personal interview, rather than in writing. We reiterate that the main purpose of a résumé is to gain an interview; it is not a substitute for an interview.

The *Functional Résumé* tends to be shorter than the *Chronological Résumé*. The example that follows has been further shortened to avoid monotonous repetition. Both the *Functional Résumé* and the *Functional-by-Company (Institution) Résumé* are well regarded by institutional recruiters.

EXAMPLE OF FUNCTIONAL RÉSUMÉ

DUNCAN SMITH
375 Broadalban Road
Ephrata, Pennsylvania 12345
(177) 377-4777

SENIOR EXECUTIVE experienced in all areas of General Management

SUMMARY OF QUALIFICATIONS

Record of consistent profit contributions amounting to millions of dollars in general management, marketing and production in the U. S. and internationally; accustomed to autonomous multi-division responsibility. Equipped to use all management techniques to accomplish company objectives.

GENERAL MANAGEMENT	Accomplished seven divisional turn-arounds leading these Divisions from high five-figure losses to six-figure profits in periods ranging from three months to two years.
PRODUCTION	Successfully engineered and produced four new products of complex technology supervising Manufacturing Manager, Controller, various engineering disciplines and marketing development.
MARKETING	Conceived and implemented new marketing plan which broadened distribution and increased volume 27%; increased profits 9%.
FINANCE	Instituted new financial controls and procedures; increased cash flow 19%; improved R. O. I. 13%; set objectives and achieved financial ratios which became envy of the industry.
TECHNICAL BACKGROUND	Intimately familiar with the metal-working industry and with sophisticated machinery and equipment in a broad area of manufacturing.

FOR FURTHER DATA PLEASE SEE FOLLOWING PAGE

DUNCAN SMITH   PAGE 2

EMPLOYMENT HISTORY

1970-Present	LEAF MANUFACTURING DIVISION, BRF, INC., Winston-Salem, N. C.
1967-1970	THOMAS & SESSIONS, Springfield, Mo.
1963-1967	W. H. THOMPSON & CO, Harrisburg, Pa.
1953-1962	VANADIUM METAL WIRE WORKS, Pittsburgh, Pa.

EDUCATION

B. S., Engineering, University of Pittsburgh, Pittsburgh, Pa.

Graduate work in Business Administration and Management at Northwestern and Michigan State Universities.

COMMUNITY ACTIVITIES

Chairman, Board of Directors, National Hospital, Winston-Salem, N. C.

Chairman, Community Chest, Winston-Salem, N. C.

Member, National Presidential Committee to Study Government Options.

HONORS

Winston-Salem Citizen-of-the-Year Award.

HOBBIES

Tennis, golf, shooting (National 12 Bore Champion)

PERSONAL DATA

Born 3/31/28, married, two children, excellent health. Willing to relocate.

REFERENCES AND FURTHER DATA ON REQUEST

DISCUSSION

Functional Résumé. Mr. Duncan Smith has experience in all four major facets of management—marketing, finance, production, and general management. The *Functional Résumé* is particularly suitable for expressing such experience. It is also suitable for one who has had the following experience:

IN MARKETING

Territory selling
Regional management
Sales or product management
Sales management

IN FINANCE

Accounting
Controller
Treasurer

IN PRODUCTION

Foreman
Superintendent
Plant manager
Director of R.&D.
General manager

IN EDUCATIONAL ADMINISTRATION

Teaching
Curriculum planning
Administration

The subject areas can be further expanded to include, for example, network techniques in production planning, other important financial ratios, and the most important markets.

EXAMPLE OF FUNCTIONAL RÉSUMÉ

78 Whitney Road   (789) 123-7654
Gastonia, N. C. 77777

R E S U M E

of

JOHN KAY

TEXTILE EXECUTIVE

Progressive career in textile industry beginning with textile education and graduation with honors, continuing with important assignments for major textile manufacturers, culminating in part ownership of specialty knitting company growing
from inception at zero to $7 million in three years. Recently sold interest in
this profitable enterprise to partners; now available for employment in the industry as Director of Marketing or Manufacturing or both.

EXPERIENCE

As General Manager:
Created company, starting with zero sales, climbing
to $ 7 million in three years, operating profitably. Di-
rected building of dye house. Started new department
for giant textile manufacturer ($800 million plus) aimed
at Men's Wear market for single and double knits.

Purchased complete equipment needed for new department (reaching $30 million volume). Established new
basis for profitable pricing.

Set up R. & D. program to promote growth.

As Director of
Manufacturing:
Departmentalized each phase of manufacturing assigning
efficiency and capacity ratings; established basis for
dependable delivery schedules. Implemented new procedures for determining true costs as basis for profitable pricing.

Initiated improved quality control. Utilized (DKJ/36 and
other) double knit pattern lock, non-jacquard and inter-
lock machines, rib transfer machines, single knit equipment 18 to 26 cut, tuck bars, wheels, raleways, plain
jerseys, finishing, dyeing and bulking equipment; with
continuous upgrading.

over please

As Marketing   Developed seasonal lines by market end-use and fiber
Manager: mix.

                          Developed special programs for key customers, presented
                          new programs and lines.

                          Created new sales programs and new advertising. Intro-
                          duced "coordinated look" in Men's Wear, achieved dom-
                          inant market position for new Division of giant textile
                          producer.

                          Maintained close "intelligence" liaison with salesmen
                          and customers.

                          EMPLOYMENT RECORD

1972-1975   NEW WEAVE COMPANY, New York, N. Y.
                          VICE PRESIDENT AND GENERAL MANAGER

1962-1972   INTERNATIONAL FABRICS, INC., New York, N. Y.
                          GENERAL MANAGER, $60 million Men's Wear Divsion

1959-1962   TERJAVIAN ET CIE, Brussels, Belgium
                          DIRECTOR OF MANUFACTURING for North Carolina mill
                          of $1 billion international knitter after earlier subordin-
                          ate experience.

MILITARY SERVICE: U. S. NAVY, 1958-1960. Served as Flight Lieutenant aboard
                          Aircraft Carrier in South China Sea.

EDUCATION: B. S., New York Institute of Textile Technology and Merchan-
                          dising, Hamilton, N. Y., 1957. Graduated Cum Laude.

                          Graduate work at Bennett University, New York, N.Y., 1958.
                          Scholarship Award from International Institute of Textile De-
                          sign.

LANGUAGES: French and Spanish (fluent).

HOBBIES: Platform tennis (ranked in first 10), skeet.

PERSONAL DATA: Age 39, married, three children, excellent health. Willing
                          to relocate.

                          REFERENCES AND FURTHER DATA ON REQUEST

DISCUSSION

Functional Résumé. The Kay résumé utilizes language appropriate to the industry. By naming the types of knitwear and knitting machinery the applicant illustrates his mastery of production techniques as well as an understanding and implementation of objectives. The marketing section shows imagination in theme development to create an important share of market.

As all other résumés in this book, this résumé shows what a successful person has done to improve job performance and how such improvement invariably contributes to the profitability and well-being of a company or institution.

The experiences related in this résumé could have been equally well expressed in other résumé styles. The *Functional* form was selected because of some inconsistencies in the chronology of employment and achievements, which would have been disadvantageously disclosed in the *Chronological* form but could easily be explained during an interview.

S E C T I O N 16

Functional-by-Company (Institution) Résumé

The Functional-by-Company (Institution) Résumé lists functions for each employer. In this respect it is superior to the *Functional Résumé*. However, the listing of functions performed for a company need not be chronological, which, though a bit misleading to the reader, may be of advantage to you. Keep in mind that a résumé is an evaluation of you. In taking "poetic license" with your chronology you may improve your résumé and gain an interview, during which discrepancies can be explained.

Preceding comments aside, the *Functional-by-Company (Institution) Résumé* is well suited for teachers and professors and is well received by academic recruiters. Two examples follow, including one for the educational area.

EXAMPLE OF FUNCTIONAL-BY-COMPANY (INSTITUTION) RÉSUMÉ

100 Accomplishment Way   Home (123) 456-7890
Erewhon, Minnesota 12345   Office (098) 765-4321

R E S U M E

HORAC ALGERIO

EXECUTIVE

SUMMARY OF QUALIFICATIONS

Experienced in all areas of management: Marketing, Production, Finance and multi-division operations. Record of consistent profit contributions in identifying and developing new markets, in creating more effective advertising themes, in reducing manufacturing costs and lead times, in reducing inventories, increasing cash flow and doubling price of common stock in a period of 12 months under adverse market conditions.

EXPERIENCE

1964-Present   GENERAL LEISURE PRODUCTS COMPANY, INC., Winona, MN.

                    1971-Present, PRESIDENT and GENERAL MANAGER with P.&L. responsibility for $100 million leisure products manufacturing division of $600 million conglomerate. Report to parent company President. Supervise Vice Presidents of Marketing, Manufacturing, Human Resources, Planning, Finance and R. & D. Department.

R. & D.   - led Research & Development team in development of new concept in grass-mowing equipment.
MARKETING   - made innovation in merchandising and advertising home snow-removal machine.
                    - utilized technology developed in mowing machinery to manufacture snowmobile; captured first place in Alaska race test.
MANUFACTURING   - selected new wholesale organization to concentrate on Company (with partial financing by Company).
                    - increased volume from $60 million to $100 million in four years.
FINANCE   - increased value of AMEX-listed stock from six to $12\frac{1}{2}$ in 1974, based on earnings multiplication.
                    - reduced inventory by one-third leading to increase in ROI.

                    1969-1971, VICE PRESIDENT, MANUFACTURING

                                                              over please

HORAC ALGERIO   PAGE 2

MANUFACTURING   - consolidated manufacture of motors in one plant heretofore
                    distributed among four plants around the U. S.
                  - closed least efficient manufacturing plant; utilized space
                    for needed new warehouse.
                  - reorganized flow of production for motors, building own
                    specialized automated equipment; reduced lead time from
                    six to three months and manufacturing cycle from two
                    months to two weeks.
                  - restyled mowers, snow removers, electric garden tools; de-
                    veloped, with R. & D., new concept in electric grass
                    shears which became nationwide best sellers and contribut-
                    ed $6 million of profitable new volume.

                  1967-1969, GENERAL MANAGER, Caracas, Venezuela

MANUFACTURING   - recognized application of new technology to manufacture of
                    small horsepower motors; increased plant productivity by
                    30%; technology adopted in three U. S. plants with similar
                    results.
GENERAL   - met with government officials to gain "favored manufacturer"
MANAGEMENT   status in Venezuela leading to lower export duties.
                  - expanded distribution to Colombia and Brazil with consequent
                    doubling of volume.
FINANCE   - reorganized accounting procedures; speeded corporate monthly
                    reports by ten days each month leading to quicker identifica-
                    tion of problem areas and increase in profits from 6% to 15%
                    before taxes.
MARKETING   - conducted market research leading to distribution of wider
                    group of U. S. manufactured products in South America,
                    with only minor changes in styling.

                  1964-1967, SALES MANAGER for U. S. and South America

MARKETING   - studied marketing procedures in the U. S. and South America.
                  - studied company potential for new products in areas of com-
                    petence.
                  - increased U. S. sales 25% through new system of regional
                    profit centers and improved training methods.
SALES   - switched main distribution efforts from traditional outlets to
                    newer forms of distribution.
                  - increased sales in South America by 15% and recommended
                    change in product mix which led to accomplishments pre-
                    viously mentioned.

1958-1964   AVERILL & HARRIMAN COMPANY, INC., Dellmore, Ill.

                  VICE PRESIDENT, MANUFACTURING for small ($40 million)
                  manufacturer of marine motors. Responsible for:

                                                            over please

         - complete manufacturing operations and R. & D. Department.

         Accomplishments:

MANUFACTURING
         - set up new production line using new automatic equipment.
         - cleared out accumulated inventory of excessive parts and raw
           material, improved turnover from three to four times annually.
         - reorganized engineering department breaking up authority into
           Quality Control, Production Control, Production Engineering,
           Methods Engineering.
         - conducted cost studies leading to 11% reduction in costs.
         - conducted value studies; made decision to purchase fasten-
           ers and other components at a saving of 16% in raw material
           costs.
         - accelerated manufacturing cycle time by 17% leading to a
           further cost reduction of 12%.

Invited by executive search firm to consider position with General Leisure Products; accepted.

1955-1958   AUTOMOTIVE PARTS, INC., Jackson, Mich.

         ASSISTANT PLANT MANAGER (one of seven) for $100 million
         manufacturer of small parts for the BIG-3 auto manufacturers.

         Learned automatic and automated production methods with one
         of most advanced companies in the industry.

MILITARY SERVICE: U. S. ARMY AIR FORCE, 1952-1955. Captain. Served in Korea.

EDUCATION: B. S., Engineering, California Institute of Technology, Pasa-
         dena, Calif., 1951. Graduate work in Business Management,
         1952, Stanford University, Stanford, Calif.

COMMUNITY   Chairman, Board of Directors, National Hospital, Winona,
ACTIVITIES: Minn.

         Chairman, Community Chest, Winona, Minn.

HONORS: Winona Citizen-of-the-Year Award

HOBBIES: Tobogganing (National Two-Man Champion), skeet, trap,
         crosscountry skiing.

PERSONAL DATA: Born 3/31/21, married, three children, excellent health.

REFERENCES AND FURTHER DATA ON REQUEST

DISCUSSION

Functional-by-Company (Institution) Résumé. The Algerio résumé illustrates how career progression can be effectively expressed using a combination of the *Functional* and the *Chronological* styles.

This applicant started in production, moved quickly to another company utilizing the production skills learned earlier, and became head of manufacturing for a medium size company. Here he demonstrated good management skills in all areas of production. He moved again to a position involving marketing to round his experience and immediately showed talent in this field, advancing quickly to general management of the company's South American division and two years later to the vice-presidency of the headquarters plant. By this time his ability in each position gave such strong indications of the highest qualities of leadership that he was appointed president of the company with results that made a strongly favorable impact on the company and its stockholders.

This is a capsule illustration not only of excellent management but also of career planning, in which the subject determined to make himself knowledgeable in all areas of management. You may here recognize a parallel to another famous career.

EXAMPLE OF FUNCTIONAL-BY-COMPANY (INSTITUTION)
RÉSUMÉ—NONPROFIT OBJECTIVE

One First Avenue   Home (212) 332-4455
Brentwood, N. Y. 54321   Office (212) 432-6688

CURRICULUM VITAE

of

SAMUEL JOHNSON

OBJECTIVE

Administrative Position with a Foundation, Educational or other non-profit organization.

EDUCATION

M. S., Education, Columbia University, New York, N. Y., 1959.

B. S., History, University of Pennsylvania, Philadelphia, Pa., 1961. Cum Laude.

Doctoral studies in Philosophy of Education.

SUMMARY OF QUALIFICATIONS

Eleven years of experience in the development of sound educational systems, administration and teaching.

HONORS

Cited in "The Last 20 Years of Education in the United States," 1st ed., (1950-
1970), Langston and Rhodes, 1971.

Named in Who's Who in Colleges and Universities, 1957, 1958, 1959.

Bronze Star in Vietnam, 1962. Silver Star, Vietnam, 1963. Captain, U. S.
Army.

over please

SAMUEL JOHNSON   PAGE 2

PUBLICATIONS

The Influence of Experimentation on Basic Learning Skills, Barnes and Dunlop, 1973, 342pp.

Basic Education in a Changing Society, Noble and Morrow, 1972, 307 pp.

Paper: A Comparison of Test Scores in Reading and Writing, Columbia University Review, 1969.

ACCREDITATIONS

Boston Board of Education, License No. 123456.

New York State Regents License No. 987654

ADMINISTRATIVE EXPERIENCE

1970-Present   OLIVER W. HOLMES UNIVERSITY, Brentwood, N. Y.

UNIVERSITY PLANNING OFFICER for University with student body of 2500 projected to rise to 3600 by 1977; faculty of 350 projected to 500 by 1977.

- Established plans for operation of University with student body expansion 1977-1987 including organization, functional responsibilities, philosophy.
- Provided plans for space needs, faculty expansion, additional courses of study, new doctoral programs, budgets, sources of income.
- Recommended enlarged emphasis on teaching skills vs. publication and outside consulting activities.

1968-1970   GOVERNOR WHEELOCK ACADEMY, West Falls, Mass.

ASSISTANT HEADMASTER for small (400 pupils) preparatory school in rural setting.

- Upgraded teaching staff.
- Supervised construction of new gymnasium.
- Participated in fund raising activities.
- Coached football and lacrosse.
- Worked with Headmaster and Board of Trustees on ten year plan for Academy.

EDUCATIONAL SYSTEMS EXPERIENCE

1966-1968   NEW YORK STATE REGENTS COMMITTEE ON CURRICULUM
                   REVISION

Invited as one of a committee of seven to study, evaluate and recommend changes in existing methods of teaching at the grade levels 7 to 12.

over please

SAMUEL JOHNSON   PAGE 3

- Instituted study of comparative reading and writing tests among 400 high schools chosen by lot in New York State; evaluated data; recommended revision in reading and remedial reading to encompass as appropriate individual student teaching, group teaching by skill levels and re-emphasis on phonetics for non-handicapped students.

- Instituted study of methods of teaching mathematics; recommended that study of "New Math" be taught in grade 12 instead of grade 9. Recommended additional emphasis on computer mathematics.

- Recommended expanded use of E. D. P. record keeping, marking, teacher evaluation, Beta system development utilizing minicomputers in specialized areas.

TEACHING EXPERIENCE

<u>1964-1966</u>   BENJAMIN FRANKLIN HIGH SCHOOL, New York, N. Y.

<u>History</u>, <u>History of Western Civilization</u>, <u>History as a Guide to the Future</u>. Developed and selected materials that were highly motivating, varied, skill directed, individualized. Rated in annual Board of Education review, "Thorough knowledge of subject". "Superior in instructional approach." "Effective in discipline."

Appointed by Principal to Policy Committee which participated in making decisions related to instruction, administration, overall school evaluations.

Helped write Federal Government proposal for creation of a teacher corps in New York City in conjunction with school district personnel, university department heads, principals and teachers.

VITAL STATISTICS

Born 3/31/39, married, three children, excellent health.

REFERENCES AND FURTHER DATA ON REQUEST

DISCUSSION

Functional-by-Company (Institution) Résumé—Nonprofit Objective. In an educational or scientific career the pertinent credentials should be given at the beginning. Though essentially *Functional-by-Company (Institution)*, the Johnson résumé starts with education and lists honors, publications, and accreditations immediately thereafter.

The career begins with teaching, proceeds to curriculum planning and to administration, and culminates in a presently held responsible position at a large university.

The job history is progressive, it has led to the formulation of an educational philosophy, and it embraces the kinds of experience most useful in performing the operating functions within the job objectives named at the outset.

Academic degrees, continuing study, an understanding of the student mind, and research in experimental and orthodox teaching methods project an individual who can contribute much to the growth and development of a nonprofit institution, particularly in academe.

S E C T I O N   17
Harvard Résumé

The *Harvard Résumé* is widely used because of its appearance and its immediate association by sophisticated readers with the Harvard Graduate School of Business Administration. It has narrow margins and long, rather informal paragraphs. The density of writing often makes it difficult to read.

Accomplishments are less sharply delineated in the *Harvard Résumé* than in other types of résumé. An unusually large amount of personal data might be given. The form usually is *Chronological*, sometimes *Functional-Chronological*.

An example of the *Harvard Résumé* follows.

EXAMPLE OF HARVARD RÉSUME

<u>RESUME</u>

James Thorpe
107 Mission Road
St. Louis, Missouri 98765
(123) 456-7890

<u>OBJECTIVE</u>

A general management or marketing opportunity where broad experience in mechanical products would be valuable. Major emphasis in background includes:

- P. & L. responsibility.

- General Management, sales management and field sales experience.

- Extensive experience with wide range of markets and new product development.

<u>EXPERIENCE</u>

Jan. 1973   WINSTON & BURDETT, INC.
   to   Harrison, Mo.
Present
            Residential division of Remington Dale Co., Inc., an independent
            sheet metal contractor, with annual volume in the range of $12 mil-
            lion, serving residential, commercial and industrial markets.

<u>Vice President</u>

Formed and autonomously manage a new division concentrating on the residential market. Sales were increased by 100% in first two years while getting new division started; earned profit from beginning amounting to 12% before taxes in second year.

Accomplishments include:

- Developing and implementing an overall business plan: market analysis; order forecasting; production plan; manpower needs and recruiting plan; training; P. & L. forecast; facilities and equipment; capital expenditure and operating capital requirements.

- Recruited and trained over 300 people.

- Developing product changes, standardized production and standard costs to achieve 16% reduction in product cost.

- Developing consumer financing plans with St. Louis and Kansas City banks to support expanded sales activities.

- Taking the organization into new product areas to expand markets and eliminate seasonal weaknesses.

1970
to
1973

SCAVER JONES DIVISION OF MARLITE, INC.
Joliet, Mo.

A $5 million manufacturer of mechanical equipment for commercial and industrial use.

General Sales Manager

Responsible for all sales through 23 independent U. S. dealers and 35 overseas distributors; with a staff of five.

Orders were increased by 20% in weakening markets which had shown a decline.

Earnings were increased through:

- price increases.

- reducing expenses through strict budget applications.

- implementing product cost reduction programs to obtain lower costs in a period of rising prices.

Also made changes in representation; set up new dealers; insitituted new training program for all dealers retained; redirected advertising.

1956
to
1970

THE CRANE COMPANY
Middletown, Mo.

A $100 million manufacturer of plumbing equipment for residential, commercial and industrial use.

Manager, Dealer Development, March 1969 to April 1970

Responsible for all Crane dealer activities to sell commercial and residential plumbing supplies. New dealers were established through company financing and long range plans for growth. This involved management of internal staff, regional staff and local office's in recruiting and training qualified personnel to own and operate dealerships. It also involved development of management skills to support business start-up at a profit.

The organization grew from 30 to 60 dealers and the sale of products from $40 to $50 million.

Manager, Dealer Distribution, March 1967 to March 1969

James Thorpe   Page 3

Responsible for managing three sales districts in the development of a dealer organization. This involved market analysis, recruiting and training.

Sales were increased from $2 million to $3 million.

Manager, Market Research, 1964-1967

Headed a marketing group to promote and sell all types of plumbing products in the industrial and wholesaler markets. Supervised marketing departments and research department. New marketing strategies and sales opportunities were created through new product and system ideas.

Sales Engineer, 1963-1964

Given responsibility to increase market share, profitability and new product development. Developed marketing program, coordinated sales and bidding strategies and trained field sales personnel.

Field Sales Engineer, 1956-1963

Sold all types of plumbing products to apartment owners, architects, contractors, industrials, wholesalers and dealers. Increased sales 230% during this period.

1952   U. S. NAVY
to
1956   Assigned to Destroyer, South China Sea. Lt. Commander

EDUCATION

University of Missouri, Columbia, Mo.

B. S. degree, Business Management, 1955

PERSONAL

Born October 12, 1933 in the small town of Hackett, Arkansas where father owned and operated a retail hardware store for more than 40 years. Married childhood sweetheart who attended University of Missouri during two of my undergraduate years. We have five lovely children including two sets of twins. I am 6' 4" in height, weigh 230 lbs. and played varsity football during my last three years at the University. Remain in excellent health.

REFERENCES AND FURTHER DATA ON REQUEST

DISCUSSION

Harvard Résumé. The Thorpe résumé features continuing career development from field sales to general management. You will note that achievement started with increases in territory sales. Management was impressed and gave the subject the opportunity to get similar results in a more responsible position. Success here led to market research management and finally to management of all dealer activities. Opportunities apparently did not come fast enough, and Mr. Thorpe moved to another company. Soon he changed employment again to obtain general management experience, so that now he is equipped for P.& L. responsibilities in addition to those in marketing. The business biographies of successful people are replete with illustrations of the desire to learn leading to employment changes—sometimes at a temporary financial sacrifice but usually to one's ultimate benefit in terms of greater success.

The *Harvard* form of résumé expresses this career exceptionally well. Note the expanded comments under personal data.

ANALYSIS OF RÉSUMÉ USERS: MARKETING

Sales management, advertising, public relations, product manager, salesman, market research. Titles range from vice-president to salesman.

The salary range (exclusive of profit sharing and fringe benefits) is $10,000 to $50,000. The median is $23,500.

In percentage:

35% earn from $27,000 to $50,000.
31% earn from $12,000 to $18,000.
30% earn from $20,000 to $26,000.
4% earn from $40,000 to $50,000.

The age range is 23 to 56.
The average age is 36.
Some 46% are in their 30s.
Females are 2.6% of the total.

Creative Résumé

The *Creative Résumé* lacks a commonly recognized form. Instead, the writer *creates* his own form. *Creative* in this sense does not necessarily mean a better résumé, but one different from the norm. Its quality and effectiveness, as always, will depend on the writer's skill.

The creativity in a *Creative Résumé* may consist in paragraphing, layout, decoration, color, method of folding, or drastically different writing—in rhyme perhaps, or with illuminated capitals, or bearing graphic forms and symbols.

Nor is a *Creative Résumé* necessarily associated with the creative professions. An artist, writer, editor, photographer, stylist, decorator, actor, musician, entertainer, entrepreneur might be drawn toward this style of résumé, but others might use it as well. Actually, too great a departure from the norm turns a résumé into a brochure. The simplified example that follows is creative only in its method of paragraphing and its objective-appraisal type of presentation. To that extent it is different, and effective.

EXAMPLE OF CREATIVE RÉSUMÉ

145 Harrison Avenue   (212) 456-7890
Rye, N. Y. 12345

RESUME

IRENE COWLES

MAGAZINE EDITORIAL DIRECTOR - EDITOR

Qualifications:	Twenty five years of successful experience as Managing Editor with unusually broad responsibilities embracing three successful magazines with a largely female readership; and as Executive Editor, Managing Editor, Features Editor, Assistant Editor in reverse chronology; with three different publishers.

> Publishers Weekly said: "The most knowledgeable woman's editor in the field." (June 1973)
>
> Magazine Writer's Digest said: "Miss Cowles has helped more aspiring writers than anyone I know." (Jan. 1970)
>
> Magazine Guild said: "Miss Cowles has identified her markets and hit them in the bull's-eye; without question one of the most talented editors in her field." (Nov. 1968)

Objective evaluation by Corporate Manpower Development Committee on Executive Evaluation:	COMPETENT in all areas of manuscript selection and purchase, production, control, organization and administration, wide author contacts and excellent reputation for judgment, decisiveness and creativity.

> Possesses in high degree ability to lead, supervise, train and gain loyalty and dedication of staff. Oriented to profitable operations.

SENSITIVE to editorial and reader needs; capable of bringing them together to gain optimum circulation and to make changes quickly as need appears. (Dec. 1970)

Employment history:	1955-1974 - National Publications, New York, N. Y.
	1949-1955 - Hillside Publishing Company, New York, N. Y.
	1948-1949 - Rex Magazine Company, New York, N. Y.
Education:	B. S., Journalism, University of Syracuse, Syracuse, N. Y., 1947.
Personal data:	Single, excellent health, no dependents, willing to relocate.

REFERENCES AND FURTHER DATA ON REQUEST

DISCUSSION

Creative Résumé.   Ms. Cowles' résumé is an excellent example of much relevant and attractive material condensed for presentation on one page. Ms. Cowles, a successful writer, was able to describe 25 years of experience in about 200 words while expressing a competence that might easily have required several pages. She has effectively made use of the words of others, permitting discussions of talents that would be ill-received if expressed subjectively.

The résumé does not follow a formal pattern and is therefore a *Creative Résumé*.

Objective statements can often be obtained from such sources as references, personnel evaluations, military evaluations, and press clippings. If well expressed, they can be used as shown in this résumé.

SECTION 19

Narrative Résumé

The *Narrative Résumé* can be a pleasing variation from formal presentations. You might use this format if you write well, including about the difficult topic of yourself, or if your background is unusual, with perhaps a strong academic foundation. The *Narrative Résumé*, because of its relative rarity, can have extra impact. Remember, however, that it will appeal to some résumé readers only.

Examples of situations in which the *Narrative Résumé* might be effective appear in this book. The form is exceptionally suitable for the *vita brevis* ("short life") type of description of one's lifework. Personal statistics and information about education, military service, hobbies, and the like can be woven into the narrative or given in a separate section.

The disadvantages of the *Narrative* form could be lack of unity, coherence, and compactness. There is also the ever-present difficulty of narrating one's personal and professional life history sufficiently objectively.

EXAMPLE OF NARRATIVE RÉSUMÉ

100 Auditorium Street   (890) 123-4567
Salt Lake City, Utah 12345

RESUME

JOHN PETER

PERSONNEL DIRECTOR/MANPOWER DEVELOPER

Born September 30, 1939, single, excellent health. Residence and travel in Belgium, France, Tanzania, Kenya, Holland, Germany, Switzerland, Italy, Tunisia, Morroco, Ivory Coast, Uganda.

Educated as follows:

M. Divinity, M. R. E., 1965, St. Christopher's Seminary, Becton, N. Y.

B. A., 1960, University of Notre Dame, South Bend, Ind.

Post Graduate:

1967, 10 months, Sociology, Louvain University, Belgium.
1966, 12 months, Sociology, Anthropology, Social Research, Princeton University, Princeton, N. J.
1964 (summer), Social Change, Social Psychology, Princeton University.
1963 (summer), Anthropology, Cross Cultural Research, Loyala University, Baltimore, Md.

Languages include: French, Spanish, Kisukuma, Kiswahili.

Hobbies include: scuba diving, mountain climbing, any racquets game.

Employment experience:

1967-1974, International Catholic Charities, New York, N. Y.

1962-1967, Extra-curricular activities while studying included: art exhibits, community relations and marriage counseling, labor negotiation, consulting, initiation of dramatized TV programs on humans relations nationally televised on Channel III, New York City.

I give the preceding statements first because they are the raw data forming the platform for my life to the present and can be tied up in a neat little package and set aside.

In 1967, acting as a Program Developer, Sociologist and Personnel Director for the Overseas Division of the International Catholic Charities, I conceived the idea of researching two African church organizations of 7000 members to ascertain the level of their functional efficiency. I was authorized to carry out such research and as a result suggested a program utilizing sociological techniques to

JOHN PETER   Page 2

provide job enrichment and stronger support of the Division by the organizations studied. My report was read with some skepticism but nevertheless the thesis was finally accepted and I was appointed to implement the suggestions made.

Essentially my suggestions involved a program of personnel reformation and membership education to serve as a model for other branches which would ultimately involve as many as 75 organizations with 60,000 membesr and 500 supervisory personnel. I spent seven years in Africa on this project in the following activities:

- clarifying the objectives and roles of leaders through re-expression in communications and seminars.
- developing a personnel policy embodying employee relationships.
- conducting role-playing sessions and strategy meetings to help bring solutions to administrative problems and improve interpersonal relationships.
- periodic evaluation of activities to assess their effectiveness.

I published the following articles during this period:

Restructuring Pastoral Programs
Catechetical Program
Youth Study Program
Attitudes in Marriage
Aspects of Communication Between Church and People
Attitudes of Youth Toward Christianity and Marriage
Attitudes of Adults Toward Christianity and Marriage
Training Manual for U. S. and African Organization Personnel

These publications were made in English and appropriate African languages.

As a result of these and related activities we enjoyed a 50% increase in membership, the program was implemented in 35 additional organizations, relationships between local and overseas personnel were improved, tensions among U. S. workers in Africa were alleviated, medical care was bettered and a library for school children was established.

I am not sure what you may think my education and experience fit me for but I wish to leave Church work to embark upon a career in business.

I think my best contributions would be made in the area of personnel although I would be willing to take any position which would be effective for you while giving me the opportunity to establish a new career.

My qualities include an understanding of and liking for people, some creativity, practical experience in working with people, a good education and an ability to conceive and implement progressive plans.

REFERENCES AND FURTHER DATA ON REQUEST

DISCUSSION

Narrative Résumé. John Peter spent about 30 years of his life in study and service contributing greatly to the expanded usefulness of his organization. At the end of that period he made a reappraisal and deciding that such service need not be a lifelong commitment, chose to try employment in the private sector. This career change required an evaluation of his past to determine the areas in which he might be most effective. His experience in dealing with people logically suggested the areas of personnel or manpower development.

Being a competent, well educated writer, but lacking business experience, Mr. Peter selected the *Narrative* form, thus notifying the reader that his was an unusual situation calling for a different approach to the job market.

As expected, the subject's obvious interpersonal communications skills, combined with an innovative mind, resulted in a successful résumé that appealed strongly to selected readers. Though without the discipline present in more formal résumés, it has the coherence, unity, logical sequence, and interest needed to make it a compelling document.

ANALYSIS OF RÉSUMÉ USERS: ADMINISTRATION

Supervision, college and school administration, public administration, foundation executives, and hospital executives.

The salary range is $8000 to $34,500.
Median salary is $14,400.
Age range is 21 to 56.
Average age is 35.
Females are 25% of the total.

S E C T I O N   20

Professional Résumé

The traditional "learned professions" are law, medicine, and theology. More broadly, a professional is one who has special knowledge enabling him to advise, guide, or instruct others. Teaching is a profession, as is any vocation requiring extensive specialized educational preparation, such as accounting, engineering, or military science.

A *Professional Résumé* therefore places initial emphasis on academic qualifications for the profession. Any other form can serve to present the balance of the information, except the *Narrative*. The most appropriate forms, however, are the *Chronological Résumé with Summary Page* and the *Functional Résumé*.

EXAMPLE OF PROFESSIONAL RÉSUMÉ

134 East 34th Street   (212) 123-5678
New York, N. Y. 10017

R E S U M E

of

EPHRAIM TUTT

ATTORNEY

OBJECTIVE: Association with law firm in general corporate and
                  securities areas, including litigation.

SUMMARY OF   Awareness of legal needs of business with ability
QUALIFICATIONS: to provide clear answers and effective remedies for
                  corporate legal problems; including litigation when
                  necessary. Intimate knowledge of the Securities
                  Act of 1933 and Exchange Act of 1934; the rules of
                  the major stock exchanges; private placements, lost
                  securities, arbitrations. Fully familiar with tax
                  laws and accounting procedures. Effective in client
                  relationships.

                  Admitted to practice in New York State and New
                  Jersey.

EDUCATION: B. A., Princeton University, Princeton, N. J., 1963.

                  J.D., University of Michigan School of Law, Ann Arbor
                  Michigan, 1967.

PERSONAL DATA: Age 30, married, two children.

PROFESSIONAL EXPERIENCE:

1973-Present   WILD, SPENCER AND KING, New York, N. Y.

ASSOCIATE with law firm.

Provide services to clients with wide range of problems but with particular
concentration on broker-dealer and specialist problems, controversies involving securities laws, sometimes leading to litigation, registrations of public
offerings with S. E. C.

- personally and successfully represented clients before N. Y. Stock Exchange,
  American Stock Exchange and S. E. C. involving disciplinary matters.

- successfully completed and closed a public offering for a corporation.

- prepared broker-dealer applications for N. Y. S. E. membership.

1969-1973   HORNBLOWER, BIDDLE CO., New York, N. Y.

ASSOCIATE HOUSE COUNSEL for major Wall Street investment banking firm.

- won arbitration involving large client of firm.

- approved many Rule 144 sales.

- successfully prosecuted or defended firm position in connection with customer claims.

- aided in drafting a compliance manual for firm; completed compliance inspection of branch offices.

1967-1969   MIDWEST STOCK EXCHANGE, Chicago, Ill.

INVESTIGATIVE ATTORNEY for Midwest Stock Exchange.

- investigated violations by member firms and their personnel of Exchange
  rules and regulations and of other regulatory agencies.

- prepared charge memoranda for prosecutions which led to disciplinary action
  by the Exchange.

- reviewed law suits and arbitrations to find if any violations existed.

REFERENCES AND FURTHER DATA ON REQUEST

EXAMPLE OF PROFESSIONAL RÉSUMÉ

Litigation Lane   (203) 100-1111
Cos Cob, Connecticut 12345

R E S U M E

of

HENRY L. ADAMS

ATTORNEY

OBJECTIVE:

"Of Counsel" relationship and general association taking advantage
of Federal Tax expertise.

SUMMARY OF QUALIFICATIONS:

Awareness of legal needs of business and ability to provide clear
answers and effective remedies for corporate legal problems.

Broad background in acquisitions and joint ventures for major corporations with record of application of fresh and sophisticated approaches to problems, and successful negotiations.

Extensive experience in general corporate work and general practice; formerly Special Attorney for I. R. S. Expertise in resolu-
tion of complex tax problems.

VITAL STATISTICS:

Born 2/29/32, married, three children.

EDUCATION:

L. L. M., 1963, Harvard University, Cambridge, MA.

L. L. B., 1956, University of Michigan, Ann Arbor, MI.

Article: "Chancery Practice and Procedure"
77 New Jersey Law Review 162

B. A., 1954, Brown University, Providence, R. I.

HENRY L. ADAMS   PAGE 2

PROFESSIONAL EXPERIENCE:

1963-Present   ALEXANDER, BOTTS & CAREY, New York, N. Y.

                        RUSKIN & GREENWOOD, New York, N. Y.

SENIOR ASSOCIATE

Experienced, both as Senior Associate with present firm and as outside General Counsel to a subsidiary of Loew's Corp., in the successful implementation
of acquisition and joint venture projects, requiring legal and business sophis-
tication, skillful negotiation and careful, often innovative restructuring and
drafting. Tax planning and imaginative project revision have been routine elements of this process. Acquisition work has included "all cash" deals,
stock for stock deals, and stock for assets with deferred payments.

Sound working relationships were established with senior executives and counsel for such corporations as Remington-Rand, American Home Products, Standard and Poor, Gimbel Bros. in implementing joint ventures and acquisitions
from letter of intent to final closing.

Experienced in corporate tax problems including accumulated earnings tax,
sales of assets, income and asset problems of REIT's, pension and profit
sharing plans, deferred compensation contracts, accounting methods, stock options, liquidations, exempt organizations, net operating loss carry-overs, re-
allocation of income, stock valuations, state and local tax problems.

In these matters, engaged in research, planning and counseling involving the
preparation of legal memoranda, opinion letters, protests and ruling requests;
negotiated with IRS at district, regional and national levels.

Experienced in general corporate work, including planning, negotiating and
drafting for incorporations, stockholders' agreements, buy-sell agreements,
employment contracts, liquidations and related minutes and resolutions. Corporate real estate work involved purchases and sales, shopping center joint
ventures, tax shelter partnership deals, options, mortgages, guarantees, etc.

Experienced in general practice matters including wills, trusts, estate plans,
general contracts, trade name and trademark agreements, franchises and matri-
monial settlements.

1959-1963   INTERNAL REVENUE SERVICE, Washington, D. C.

SPECIAL ATTORNEY, Office of General Counsel. Primary responsibility involved
representing the Government in tax disputes:

- Settlement negotiations with corporate and individual taxpayers and determina-
  tion of whether to settle or litigate.

- Preparation of pleadings, motions, subpoenas, stipulations, briefs and other
  documents for cases pending before Tax Court.

HENRY L. ADAMS   PAGE 3

 - Conducting trial cases in Tax Court.

COMMENDATIONS:

"The Lawyer's Lawyer gratefully acknowledges the contribution of Henry L.
Adams to continuing legal education in the U. S. by reason of his authorship
of the article, 'Syndications: Federal Tax Aspects', published in the Lawyer's
Lawyer, April 1973.

Chief Counsel, U. S. Treasury Department, IRS:

"I would like to take this opportunity to express my appreciation for the splen-
did work you have performed for this office. . ."

Judge of the Circuit Court of the U. S.:

"I can say without reservation that Mr. Adams has been an effective advocate
for the Commissioner in extremely complex cases where the petitioners are represented by highly skilled attorneys. . ."

ADDITIONAL PROFESSIONAL ACTIVITIES:

Books:

   Federal Tax Manual: three volume set of tax annotated form books, approximately 3,000 pages.

   Successful Underwriting for New Companies, 550 pages.

   Connecticut Law Journal: ". . . an excellent working tool for the legal
   practitioner in acquainting himself with all aspects affecting the public issue and sale of securities of a business enterprise . . ."

   New Jersey Law Journal: "This work is recommended particularly for the
   day-to-day practical workings of the business lawyer who needs a quick,
   good, reliable reference . . ."

   Revision Editor of Moody on Wills.

Articles:

   On various corporate tax problems, published in 1958, 1959 and 1964.

MEMBERSHIPS:

American Bar Association

New York Bar Association

REFERENCES AND FURTHER DATA ON REQUEST

DISCUSSION

Professional Résumés. The two preceding résumés give objective first and a summary of qualifications second, with education and personal data following thereafter. In the Tutt résumé experience is more limited than in the Adams résumé, in which more detail was therefore incorporated. Both attorneys illustrate their backgrounds with excellent examples that are, as would be expected, consistent with their objectives. Considerable research was needed to select the most relevant and significant cases from scores or hundreds of them.

Both résumeś show individuals of considerable expertise, capable of bringing exceptional abilities to any firm.

Note the inclusion of objective commendations and a listing of publications where applicable.

ANALYSIS OF RÉSUMÉ USERS: PRODUCTION

Plant manager, production manager, inventory control, quality control, and the various engineering disciplines.

The salary range is $10,500 to $28,000.
The median is $19,500.
The age range is 31 to 58.
The average age is 45.
Age in percentages

35% are in their 40s.
37% are in their 50s.
16% are in their 30s.

There are no females in the survey.

Accomplishment Résumé

The *Accomplishment Résumé* lists accomplishments without reference to dates and companies and without regard for a chronological order. It is often used by individuals who wish to disguise age, length of experience, employment gaps, lack of progress in recent jobs, job-hopping, and other matters that are easier to explain in person during an interview than in writing. Do not let these reasons dissuade you from using this form if you like it, however. Some nonprofit executive employment services favor this style.

The elements of the *Accomplishment Résumé* are the following:

1. Name, address, and telephone number.
2. Summary of qualifications.
3. List of accomplishments (the most important is given first).
4. List of companies by whom employed (no dates).
5. Military service (no dates).
6. Education (no dates).
7. Hobbies, professional memberships, community activities, and honors (no dates).
8. Personal data (omit age).

An example of the *Accomplishment Résumé* follows.

EXAMPLE OF ACCOMPLISHMENT RÉSUMÉ

221-B Baker Street   (123) 456-7890
Sherlock, Va. 12345

JOHN MILTON

OPERATIONS EXECUTIVE

* * *   Experienced manager with proven record of accomplishments in creating profits and often innovative solutions to corporate problems, representing tens of millions of dollars.

* * *   Record of progress to increasingly important responsibilities in every employment. Accustomed to working with and leading staffs in improving systems and procedures, in developing harmonious labor relations, in organizing projects for most efficient completion.

* * *   Excellent in written and oral communication with wealth of experience in construction, maintenance, site selection, leasing, facilities planning, display, floor layout, contract negotiation, organization of diverse departments involving multi-million dollar programs.

* * *   Experience in the activities enumerated has been world-wide.

FOR FURTHER DATA PLEASE SEE FOLLOWING PAGE

JOHN MILTON   PAGE 2

ACHIEVEMENTS:

Cost saving of $1 million in one year using reduced level of personnel and no loss of efficiency.

Completed $50 million construction project in five months with four general contractors saving Company from financial difficulty.

Saved $35,000 annually by devising new method of inventory control.

Set up central purchasing for ten units saving 13% on annual purchases of $12 million.

Planned, coordinated and supervised a multimillion dollar construction project with cost saving of $183,000 and bonus to contractor for beating deadline by two weeks.

Planned new housewares department (100,000 sq. ft.) for increased traffic and improved merchandise visibility without loss of business during reconstruction.

Saved 12% in electricity and fuel in group of 37 nationally-known department stores saving more than $3 million in annual costs.

Reduced cost of new two million sq. ft. warehouse 25% by creating flexible storage locations, making changes in rack specifications and other creative planning.

Reduced insurance costs for a three million sq. ft. building by a program of continuous maintenance.

Consolidated insurance on a national basis at a cost saving of $10 million over a period of two years.

Devised new security methods that reduced shoplifting and other causes of loss by 75% with a resultant saving of $13 million. And more.

The preceding accomplishments were achieved for the following companies:

Great Atlantic and Caribbean Coffee Company, Vice President.

The International Insurance Companies, Vice President Operations.

Allied Retailers, Incorporated, Buildings Manager.

Hughes Construction Company, Field Engineer.

EDUCATION: B. S., Rice University, Houston, Texas.

PERSONAL DATA: Married, 3 children, excellent health. Willing to relocate.

REFERENCES AND FURTHER DATA ON REQUEST

DISCUSSION

Accomplishment Résumé. The material in the Milton résumé was condensed from another résumé of about four pages to two for purposes of illustration. It suffers from a lack of relationship between achievements and employers and lack of explanation of work methods (such as determining the flow of information from the point of sale to the computer, making time studies of jobs, and so forth), which would have added greatly to an understanding of this man's value and the reasons for some of his assignments. Nevertheless, it is effective in presenting a man whose every assignment has been so successful that an employer in need of such skills would be inclined to interview him.

Actually the original résumé, written in *Chronological* form, was very impressive. A broadcast letter summary elicited replies from 70% of the companies approached—an unusually high percentage. Not all replies, largely from the top officers, resulted in interviews, but they provided a base for aggressive follow-ups, leading to personal interviews.

S E C T I O N   22

Getting Ready to Write Your Résumé

All the preceding sections in this book have been preparing you for writing your résumé. The key to this task is the analysis and orderly listing of your job responsibilities and achievements. You must know yourself: what you were or are expected to do, what you actually did or are doing, and how your action affected your job, your section, your department, your division, or your company or organization.

To help you organize these facts, we have prepared an analytical questionnaire. We suggest that you use it. It has been carefully set up so as to make you think about yourself, recall forgotten activities, and focus on actions instrumental in your vocational life. You must first recall events, and then describe your recollections. The second task is eased if done after you have performed the first. Jot down the things that you have accomplished in the form of informal notes, using single words, phrases, and sentence fragments. These notes will serve as the basis for the actual résumé.

SIX BASIC STEPS

Follow these six basic steps in writing your résumé:

1. Assemble the raw data (from your answers to our analytical questionnaire).
2. Refine the data (initial draft).
3. Select the most relevant data.
4. Translate the data into suitable language. Your sentences and paragraphs are the building blocks that you can move around to fit your chosen résumé form.
5. Select your résumé format.
6. Write your résumé.

YOUR ANALYTICAL QUESTIONNAIRE

Before starting on your résumé, gather the data for it by answering the analytical questionnaire below. Your answers will serve to give your résumé focus, direction, and the proper "slant." If you have difficulty in answering a question, skip it for now and return to it later. Take plenty of time to think about yourself and to make a thoughtful self-analysis. Depending on your background, completing the questionnaire will require a half hour to several hours.

1. Your name, address, and home and office telephone numbers.
2. Titles of jobs desired, if possible. If you cannot supply them at this time, briefly *describe* the job you want. Identify several jobs by assigning to them the letters A, B, C, and so on, using the same code in Question 3 below.

   Turn to Question 11 and answer it before answering the questions that follow.
3. Qualifications that you believe you should have for the jobs A, B, C, and so on, listed in Question 2. (Most data should be in answer to Question 11.) *For example,* your answer to Question 2 is "sales manager," you might answer the present question as follows:

    a.   Appraise pricing and distribution policies.
    b.   Recruit and train sales staff.
    c.   Maintain distributor liaison.
    d.   And so on.

Now *underline* the qualifications you have *and* list any other qualifications you feel you should have for the jobs you desire.

4. Your age, marital status, number of children, home ownership, car ownership, and so on.
5. Military service

    a.   Dates, branch of service, rank.
    b.   Special training, courses, responsibilities.

6. Education—dates, schools, academic degrees, and proficiency in languages.
7. Major and minor courses. List courses relevant to the jobs desired. State your class standing if possible. Describe scholarships, awards, and honors.
8. Extra-curricular activities at school (sports, jobs, social activities, etc.).
9. Hobbies and your degree of proficiency in them, travel (if extensive), memberships in societies and community activities.
10. A summary of your employment history. *Work backwards,* giving the last job first. Use three columns to assemble the following information:

Dates of beginning job and
leaving job (years only)   Company and address   Job
titles

11. For each job listed above, starting with the *last* job, give the following data. Treat each position or important assignment with the same company, or with important clients of your employer, as though it were a separate and distinct job. Answer *each* question carefully.

    a.   Job title.
    b.   Dates of beginning and leaving job (by transfer to another company or by promotion or change within a company).
    c.   Beginning and ending salaries or earnings.
    d.   Name of company and division or department within company.
    e.   Description of what the company makes, sells, or does.
    f.   An indication of size of company—by sales volume, number of employees, number of plants, and number of branches or stores, for example.

g.   The title of the person for whom you worked (president, foreman, sales manager, etc.).
h.   The number of persons you supervised (if any).
i.   The kinds of employees you supervised (engineers, clerks, etc.).
j.   The types of equipment you used (or that was used under your supervision) and for what purpose. This will be relevant for such jobs as production manager and computer executive, but irrelevant for others.
k.   Your responsibilities. Describe them briefly but fully; give facts, rather than abstract generalities. Consult page 16, Section 9 under "Experience" before answering this question.
l.   Your accomplishments. Describe them briefly but specifically.

- The problems you were faced with.
- What you did about them.
- What you achieved and how.

That is, what did you see that needed to be done, what did you do about it, and what happened as a result? Do not list mere claims, such as "I increased sales." Give facts: "I found that sales were only $150,000. I made a market survey and determined that the market needed a "widget." I introduced a new line of widgets. I trained salesmen by doing X Y Z. Sales increased in six months by $50,000." Such an analysis is important. You need it in your résumé if you are to stand out from other job applicants. It will also reassure you that you are qualified for the job you want, in addition to refreshing your memory and providing valuable *rehearsal and training* for your job interviews.

12.   References: name, title, company, address, and telephone number (and extension). Do not include references in your résumé; assemble them for use at interviews.

GUIDANCE IN ANSWERING THE QUESTIONNAIRE

The two sample answers to this questionnaire appearing below illustrate what you should *not* do. Here is how one man answered Question 11:

1972-present (name of company). AREA SUPERVISOR. Began February 1972 as restaurant manager in failing unit. The unit started to show profit after four weeks. I was promoted to supervisor of two units after three months. In the following months I was given the entire Maryland area to supervise (five units). A new type of concept was developed, and I was picked to bring it into a profitable operation. At that point the larger volume (Philadelphia) units were given to me to supervise. At my request, I was moved to the New York area as supervisor in July 1973. Since that time I have opened three large volume units for the chain, both in New York and in Pennsylvania. All of the six units now under my supervision gross $1 to $1.5 million per year.

This very successful man needed much prodding before supplying additional information vital to his case. In the final résumé below the portions with data initially not disclosed are underlined.

1972–present (name of company)

AREA SUPERVISOR for a rapidly growing, limited menu, full service, $30 million AMEX-listed restaurant chain with 30 locations; earlier single unit manager. Responsible for New York and Pennsylvania area supervising six $1 to $1½ million units each with a staff of 60 to 90 people.

— Indoctrinated company with new cost concepts which have contributed significantly to rapid growth from nine units in 1971 to 30 units currently.
— Reduced food cost from 40% to 35%.
— Opened three large volume units: hired, trained complete staffs, installed systems.
— Accustomed to exercising controls through analysis of computer printouts daily on food, liquor, payroll. Trained managers in use of cost analyses.

Earlier managed failing unit; turned it from loss to profit in four weeks by exercise of proper controls, by establishing incentive system, and by gaining cooperation of employees. Personally contributed to success of 15 of existing 30 units and set standards for entire operation.

Prod yourself for the type of detail that, as just demonstrated, can turn a poor résumé into an effective one. What did you see that needed to be done? In this case the corporation was in need of profitability. What did you do about it? In this case the man created better cost concepts. What happened as a result? In this case the units became profitable.

In our second example of how *not* to answer the analytical questionnaire the subject took a shortcut. The result again was the omission of vital information.

1. John Abrams, 367 Pasadena Ave., Pasadena, Calif. Home (123) 456-7890. Office (321) 654-0987.
2. Sales manager.
3. a. Styling of line.
    b. In charge of all shipping.
    c. Distribution of goods to the factory—what goes into work at the machines.
    d. Production.
4. 36—married—3 children—own home and car.

5. U.S. Naval Reserve 1956–1964—2 years active—6 years reserve.
6. High school graduate—4 years—with some college.
7. Academic.
8. Worked in specialty shop—worked in bowling alley. Sports—bowling, football, baseball, horseback riding.
9. Horseback riding, photography.
10. Seventeen years in the employ of Toni Co., 1958–1975.
11. a. Sales manager.
    b. 1958–1975.
    c. $45 week to $560 week.
    d. Sales department.
    e. Ladies' ready-to-wear.
    f. 35 employees—$4,500,000.00.
    g. President.
    h. Supervised up to 10 employees.
    i. Salesmen, shipping clerks, production workers.
    j. Sewing machines, cutting machines, taping machines.
    k. Making sure all machines were running in proper order. Responsible for putting them in proper order if not working. Selling, getting orders by phone out of town. Getting merchandise from the factory in time to ship goods. Getting piece goods in on time as per delivery order. Consistently, I had to be after these people to get the goods I needed to run the business in a proper manner.
    l. In the 17 years I was with the company, I worked up from delivery boy to sales manager. The achievement of being able to book $1.0 to $1.21 million a year.

The man omitted the following important information:

1. Business increased from $2 million to $3.5 million during his tenure.
2. The business was discontinued because of the owners' retirement.
3. The company had a sales showroom in conjunction with the factory, where he accomplished a lot of selling to out-of-town buyers.
4. He was in charge of purchasing, inventory control, and sales forecasting and was production manager in addition to being sales manager.
5. He supervised seven salesmen operating nationally and reported to the president.
6. His association with buyers was such that he could book large orders by telephone.
7. He was an excellent salesman himself, in addition to successfully managing a sales organization.
8. He personally sold to most of the major Los Angeles and other West Coast department stores and was responsible for getting business from such national accounts as Sears, Ward, and Penney.

The final résumé, with all information included, follows.

CHRONOLOGICAL RÉSUMÉ WITH SUMMARY PAGE

367 Couture Avenue   Home (123) 456-7890
Pasadena, California 12345   Office (432) 654-0987

R E S U M E

of

JOHN ABRAMS

SALES MANAGER - APPAREL

***   Seventeen years of experience in apparel field with one com-
           pany, for last ten years as Sales Manager, responsible for
           increasing multimillion dollar business by 75%. Owners re-
           tired and business was terminated.

***   Close associations with leading buyers of women's dresses
           and pants suits all over the United States, experienced in
           selling to department and specialty stores, chains, giant na-
           tional retailers and in maintaining productive contacts with
           major buying offices.

***   Effective trainer and leader accustomed to managing national
           sales organization. Management versatility led to expanded
           responsibilities including production, purchasing, shipping and
           assistance in styling and pricing in addition to marketing.

***   Excellent personal salesman with ability to get and retain cus-
           tomer loyalty and write business either by personal calls or by
           telephone, with hundreds of leading buyers across the country.

***   Capable of bringing additional volume and profit to any women's
           wear manufacturer.

FOR FURTHER DATA PLEASE SEE FOLLOWING PAGE

JOHN ABRAMS   PAGE 2

BUSINESS EXPERIENCE:

1958-1975   TONI COMPANY, Los Angeles, California

SALES MANAGER for $4.5 million manufacturer of Women's Apparel with show-room and factory in California; sold nationally to department and specialty stores, chains and such giant retailers as Sears, Ward and Penney. Supervised staff of seven salesmen and Production Manager. Reported to President. Owners decided to retire and business was terminated. Responsible for:

- developing increased sales through leadership and training of seven salesmen, and personal selling.
- sales forecasting, inventory control, purchase of piece goods and trimmings. ·
- aiding in pricing and styling.
- expediting production as necessary to achieve prompt shipments.

Accomplishments:

- rose from delivery boy to Sales Manager with earnings increases to 12 times starting salary.
- increased volume 87%; opened scores of new customers; developed existing customers.
- personally accounted for sales of $1.0 million to $1.25 million annually to leading accounts around the country.
- improved turnover by rigid inventory controls.
- curtailed price increases by creative piece goods purchasing.

MILITARY SERVICE:

1956-1964   U. S. NAVAL RESERVE. Two years active duty; Airman 3rd Class.

EDUCATION:

Three years at University of California in Los Angeles.

EXTRA-CURRICULAR ACTIVITIES:

Worked while attending high school and college; participated in football, lacrosse, bowling, riding.

HOBBIES:

Riding, photography.

PERSONAL DATA:

Age 36, divorced, two children.

REFERENCES AND FURTHER DATA ON REQUEST

ANALYSIS OF RÉSUMÉ USERS: RETAIL

Assistant buyers, buyers, merchandise managers, store owners, retail advertising, display executives, and store managers.

The salary range is $10,000 to $52,000.
Median salary is $23,500.
Average age is 40.5.
Females are 11% of the total.

S E C T I O N   23

Writing Your Résumé

To begin with, turn to *your* answers to Question 11 in the analytical questionnaire. Write your résumé first in the *Chronological* form. Write dates of employment (beginning and ending) for the most recent position. Write name of company for which you work (or worked).

Write your title and describe briefly what the company does. Write in the first person, but avoid the use of "I." Describe each responsibility concisely, in a brief, almost terse, sentence or phrase. Omit responsibilities that are unimportant or negative with respect to your objective. For example, if clerical chores are part of your job as an office manager, make no mention of them if your job objective is "office manager." Now briefly and clearly write your achievements. Emphasize contributions to profit, cost savings, new techniques or methods you introduced, mechanical or product improvements, training programs, departmental reorganizations, accuracy, and anything else about you that is positive.

What did you do and what happened as a result? To answer these questions, use the words that are best understood in your field, but avoid overly technical language (study the résumé examples included in this book, as well as the vocabulary section) in Appendix B. Use simple words wherever possible if they say exactly what you mean. For example, the employment of a computer programmer, recommended by the department head, may require the approval of a higher level executive. The chances are that the executive is unfamiliar with computer jargon, but he *will* wish to know whether you can communicate your special expertise to nonspecialists. Such terms as FORTRAN, COBOL, and second, third, and fourth generation identification numbers are all fine, but use them sparingly.

Follow this procedure for each position that you have held. The most recent jobs are usually the most important ones. "Most recent" may mean the past year for a young person or the preceding 10 to 15 years for an older person. Give most space to the areas of your greatest accomplishments. Account for time back to your earliest jobs, unless they are completely irrelevant. For example, if you have been a city administrator for several years, it is unimportant that you were a waiter or a porter at some previous time. Several years can be bunched together as "1954–1959, various unrelated positions as bookkeeper, cost analyst, station agent, prizefighter."

After your business, professional, or other vocational experience list military service. An outstanding military career would require a detailed description; dates, service arm, and rank will suffice for an average one.

Education, extracurricular activities, community activities, awards, personal data, and others follow, as discussed elsewhere and as exemplified in the many résumé samples in this book.

As a final sentence add "References and further data on request."

If you wish to add a summary paragraph or page describing your accomplishments in functional terms first review the accomplishments sections of your résumé and your answers to Question 3 in the analytical questionnaire. Suppose that you have described your accomplishments as follows:

a. Promoted to manage larger office which was operating at a loss.
b. Increased sales from $5.0 million to $7.8 million.
c. Reduced staff of sales managers from 8 to 2.
d. Brought operation from loss to profit.
e. Assigned to another losing office to attempt similar recovery.

Your front page summary might then read like this:

Assigned successively to branches operating at a loss. Consistently successful in creating profitability in every position, increasing sales and revenues variously from 60% to more than 100%, and reducing costs by streamlining management.

Or you might have made the following listing of accomplishments.

a. Assigned to manage new venture; set up new corporation.
b. Went from groundbreaking to startup in five months, one month ahead of schedule.

   c. Worked within forecasted capital and expense budgets.

   d. Wrote off all startup expenses and put company in a profit position within five months of startup and three months ahead of schedule.

   e. Increased profit from 35% to 40%.

   f. Developed cost reducing shift schedules, fringe benefit packages; improved productivity.

   g. Program influenced the establishment of a second profitable subsidiary.

This front page summary might then be in order:

Experience as general manager includes all areas of responsibility from original incorporation, site selection, building design and construction, and hiring and training to startup and operation; all work consistently ahead of schedules.

Record of profitability improvement from increased revenues. Cost savings by innovative planning in connection with work scheduling and worker incentive packages. Set viable precedent for further profitable corporate expansion.

Review the *Chronological Résumé with Summary Page* annotated for additional explanation of résumé layout and the preparation of a summary page or paragraph. Under this setup you are essentially turning specific accomplishments into a more generalized description of what you did. That is, you are using specific accomplishments as the basis for an expressive summary—if you increased profits from 35% to 40% (specific) you are a manager who can add profitability to a corporate activity (functional).

A correctly written résumé should flow, one action or achievement leading to the next. You had certain responsibilities. As a result you took certain actions. The actions were of such and such a nature. They culminated in the results described. The results saved time and money. Additional profits were created, morale was improved. Each assignment for a company or a succession of companies brought increased responsibilities. Results were progressive or forward moving.

This evolutionary development of a career is best shown in the *Chronological Résumé* or the *Chronological Résumé with Summary Page.*

EXAMPLE OF A RÉSUMÉ TYPED ON BORDERED PAPER

100 Bay Boulevard   Home (123) 456-7890
San Francisco, California 96017   Office (321) 098-7654

R E S U M E

of

ANNE BOLEYN

RESEARCH AND SAMPLING STATISTICIAN

* * *   More than 12 years of experience in statistical research,
          sampling, systems design, in supervisory capacities and in
          personnel management with recognition for contributions to
          more efficient departmental operations and more effective
          marketing planning.

* * *   Developed unique statistical system for reducing calls to non-
          operating telephone numbers derived by random computer gen-
          eration.

* * *   Identified share of market gains and losses for important
          clients resulting in vital adjustments to marketing approach.

* * *   Experienced in statistical techniques for probability samples,
          demographic studies, forecasting, budgeting, economic pro-
          jections; in working with leading consultants when necessary;
          act as consultant within areas of competence.

* * *   M. B. A. and B. A. Degrees, age 34, married.

FOR FURTHER DATA PLEASE SEE FOLLOWING PAGES

S E C T I O N   24
Typing Your Résumé

Type your résumé on good quality (16 to 20 pound weight) bond paper 8½ by 11 inches in size. The IBM Executive and the Selectric typewriters have attractive, readable typefaces. Reproduce your résumé by offset printing to retain its good appearance. The sheet can be folded in various ways to obtain a "different look." We prefer standard size and format, using *content* and *language* to create an exceptional résumé.

White, unembellished paper is best, though a blue legal backing or simple colored borders can be attractive. Whether you are an artist, writer, graphics specialist, or government administrator, the person reading your résumé most wants to know what you can contribute to the company or organization in profit, leadership, initiative, reliability, and the like. As an artist or designer you might best expend your effort in preparing a superior work portfolio rather than in embellishing your résumé. Do not use conformed right-hand margins. Keep the résumé neat, but informal in a nonprofessional format.

Use short sentences. Observe grammatical rules and conventions. Punctuate for readability. Use underlining and uppercase letters for emphasis.

Keep paragraphs short. Double or triple space between paragraphs. It is easier to read a properly spaced résumé of three or four pages than one page of closely written, overcrowded copy.

The physical appearance (format) of your résumé matters very much. Typing, layout, margins, headlines, centering, paragraphing, spacing, spelling, punctuation—all have bearing on the effectiveness of your résumé. Poorly done, they wreck a good résumé. Well done, they enhance a poor one.

Choose the format that you consider to be the most appealing from the many résumé examples in this book. Some specific guidelines for typing your résumé and your summary page are given below.

RÉSUMÉ

Allowing 1 inch from the top of the page, type your name in uppercase letters at the left margin. The page number, indicated by an uppercase PAGE and an arabic numeral, is placed on the same line at the right margin.

Triple space before the first category, "EXPERIENCE." Each category is typed in uppercase letters.

Double space and type date of employment of last job at left margin. Company name and address are typed in uppercase letters on the same line at approximately the center of the page.

Double space and start the job description, with the job titles in uppercase letters. The body is single spaced with double spacing between paragraphs and categories.

After the last category and description, triple space and center the phrase, "REFERENCES AND FURTHER DATA ON REQUEST," in uppercase letters.

Choice of margins, positioning of headlines, paragraphing, use of dashes and asterisks, and spacing are largely aesthetic matters.

SUMMARY PAGE

Starting approximately 1 inch from the top of the page at the left margin, type your home address. Your home (and business) telephone number is typed on the same line at the right margin. Margins should be at least ½ inch wide.

The word "RÉSUMÉ" typed in uppercase letters is centered 5 or 6 lines below the last line of the address. Double space and write the word "of" in lowercase letters (centered). Double space and center the name in uppercase letters. Double space again and center in uppercase letters the position title or objective.

Triple space and type a dividing double line to separate the heading from the body of the summary page.

Triple space and indent each paragraph, setting it off with triple asterisks.

Center paragraphs on the page, with triple spacing separating single spaced paragraphs.

Leave three or more spaces (depending on the position on the page of the last paragraph) before centering the phrase (in uppercase letters) "FOR FURTHER DATA, PLEASE SEE FOLLOWING PAGES."

COMPARISON OF PICA AND ELITE TYPES

The pica type appearing on the Executive typewriter requires about 18% more space, double spaced, than does the elite type. A typewritten page with 1 inch margins at top and bottom would show a difference of 2 inches between the two type sizes. Three inches take in about eight lines of Executive type and nine lines of elite type in double spaced copy. Three more lines of elite type than of pica type would fit into a 9 inch space. Single spacing doubles the number of lines. The size of paragraph indentations will affect these estimates.

EXAMPLE OF PICA TYPE (THE EXECUTIVE TYPEWRITER)

Almost all successful corporations use advertising as one of their basic techniques for building business and improving profitability. A resume is an individual's method of advertising him or herself; perhaps the only method of advertising for the great majority. Some people hire public relations firms to gain an image; some have important or newsworthy accomplishments that place their names in the news media. Most must rely on a resume to circulate information about their talents or expertise.

In writing about oneself it is best to be dignified and professional. The modern resume has evolved as a rather formal document. At its best it is concise, informative and literate. Unlike a novel it cannot use the devices of plot, humor, imagination and length to create and resolve situations. It is real and subject to the

EXAMPLE OF ELITE TYPE

Almost all successful corporations use advertising as one of their basic techniques for building
business and improving profitability. A resume is an
individual's method of advertising him or herself;
perhaps the only method of advertising for the great
majority. Some people hire public relations firms
to gain an image; some have important or newsworthy
accomplishments that place their names in the news
media.

In writing about oneself it is best to be dignified and professional. The modern resume has evolved
as a rather formal document. At its best it is concise, informative and literate. Unlike a novel it
cannot use the devices of plot, humor, imagination
and length to create and resolve situations. It is
real and subject to the infirmities that each of us
has and to the limitations of time, space and honesty.
These limitations require the discipline of formal-
ity. Add to this the difficulty of self expression
and you find another reason to have and follow rules
of procedure. That is what this book is all about.

S E C T I O N   25

The Covering Letter

Your résumé, when mailed, should be accompanied by a covering letter. It should be dated. The covering letter is a way of introducing yourself, saying what you want, and asking for an answer. Keep it brief, quickly leading to that all important document—your résumé.

It is appropriate to write a special covering letter for any résumé being sent to someone you know or with respect to a job about which you have some knowledge. You can adjust a covering letter to fit a particular person or job while a résumé cannot be that frequently revised. Address such a special letter to a specific person, with the proper title, address, and salutation.

For a general mailing a general letter is suitable. Though it is always better to address a letter to a specific person, the salutations "Dear Sir" or "Gentlemen" are acceptable in a general letter. Filling in a name might be impossible in a printed letter because of the difficulty of matching typefaces.

Your covering letter identifies you:

After 14 years as sales manager of a major company in the lighting industry during which time I was instrumental in increasing sales 27%, I am now qualified for full marketing responsibilities in or outside this industry. My résumé discloses the nature and depth of my experience.

It asks for an interview:

I would like to discuss with you how I can be productive for your company while at the same time creating a satisfactory career for myself.

It requests an answer:

I look forward to your reply.

Sincerely,

John Smith

A covering letter may also serve as a summary of qualifications if they do not appear in the résumé. We suggest, however, that the covering letter be kept informal and brief, letting the résumé convey your message.

Type the covering letter on a sheet of 8½ by 11 inches, or 7 by 10 inches if the letter is short. Name and address, appearing at the top, can be engraved, in raised letters, printed, or typed. Engraved or printed stationery is preferred, but not essential if you are short on money or time (getting stationery printed can take several weeks).

A résumé that is weak because one's accomplishments cannot be suitably expressed, can be strengthened by a covering letter describing latent abilities, aspirations, and personal qualities that have no place in the résumé itself but might help to obtain an interview.

A disability—one eye, a limp, an arthritic hand, a speech defect, eye sensitivity to bright lights, or anything else that might be noted by an interviewer—should be mentioned in the covering letter so that both you and the interviewer are prepared in advance. Your disabilities are not necessarily a disadvantage, and may sometimes be described in a manner that creates added interest.

Unsolicited letters should be addressed to the most appropriate individual within a company:

1. In a small company it is usually the president or owner who makes or approves all employment decisions.
2. In a larger company send middle management inquiries to the executive in charge of your departmental area (sales, finance, production) or to the personnel director.
3. For a position at the entry level in a medium size or large company address your letter to the personnel director.
4. If you know someone in the company you are approaching, send your letter to that person.
5. If you are an upper level executive with unusual qualifications use a broadcast letter instead of a résumé with covering letter and address it to the top executive or one of the top executives by name.
6. At the clerical level send your letter to the attention of the personnel department.
7. If your case is unusual (you are changing careers, for example) or if you have special credentials (education, background, military career) that you think would be of interest to a top executive, send the covering letter and résumé to him or her. Your letter will be routed to the proper department head.
8. If you are interested in working in a particular department, send your covering letter and résumé to the head of that department, rather than the personnel department.

When addressing a corporation, use the salutations "Dear Sir" or "Gentlemen." When addressing an individual, use his or her name and title, as shown below. Information about unusual forms of address can be found in most dictionaries.

Mr. John Smith, President
Roland Smith Co., Inc.
1 Bridge Street
Cohama, Nevada

Dear Mr. Smith: [or]   Dear Sir:

Roland Smith Co., Inc.
1 Bridge Street
Cohama, Nevada

Gentlemen: [or]   Attn: Mr. John Smith

Mrs. John Smith, President
Roland Smith Co., Inc.
1 Bridge Street
Cohama, Nevada

Dear Mrs. Smith: [or]   Dear Madam:

Ms. Eleanor Smith, President
Roland Smith Co., Inc.
1 Bridge Street
Cohama, Nevada

Dear Ms. Smith:

In typing your covering letter, place the date three lines below the last line of the letterhead (the heading containing your name and address), slightly to the right of the center of the page.

Start the address four or five lines (or more if the letter is short) below the date, at the extreme left margin.

Salutation starts on the third line after the address.

Double space before typing the body of the letter. The letter text is single spaced, with double spacing between paragraphs. When completed, the body of the letter should be centered on the page, with all margins being equal.

Double space between the body of the letter and the complimentary close. The complimentary close should be aligned with the date.

The name (aligned with the complimentary close) is typed five spaces below, allowing sufficient room for the signature.

Reference initials of the writer are indicated on the same line as the typed signature at the extreme left margin, typed in uppercase letters.

Examples and a layout of a covering letter appear below. The first letter is typed with a *block margin*, that is, without indentations. *Indented* margin means that the first line of each paragraph is indented.

A COVERING LETTER

R. D. Goethals
20 Broad Street
Trenton, N. J. 07964
(201) 123-8765

Dear Sir:

The enclosed resume will be of interest to you for your recently advertised engineering opening.

I will be glad to discuss in further detail how my experience could be utilized. Since I have been a successful profit-oriented negotiator at Project and Program levels, my main area of interest would be in support and engineering, contract administration and problem solving.

Please 'phone or write to me suggesting a suitable time for a personal interview.

Sincerely,

RD   R. D. Goethals

A COVERING LETTER IN ANSWER TO A DISPLAY ADVERTISEMENT

Cornelia Ryan
100 Winding Way
Oklahoma City, Oklahoma 12345
(123) 456-7890

Mr. Giles Blass, President
Automatic Equipment Company
Industrial Park
Dallas, Texas 34567

Dear Sir:

In re: your advertisement the <u>Wall Street Journal</u>, 3/30/74 –

I am a personnel executive with eight years of achievement and increasing responsibilities.

I am expert in personnel administration, training, labor relations and executive recruiting.

My resume is enclosed.

May I discuss with you how I might be contributory to your Company? I look forward to your reply.

Sincerely,

CR   Cornelia Ryan

A GENERAL LETTER INTRODUCING A RÉSUMÉ

Olympic Towers, Apt. 30
127 East 60th Street
New York, N.Y. 10000

The Adam Bede Co.
100 Rural Road
Claremont, N.Y. 10000   Attn: V.P. Personnel

Gentlemen:

    With intensive experience for more than fifteen years in all facets of financial management, operations and support systems for management and a record of consistent profit contributions, I am qualified for a senior management position in operations or finance.

    Please review my resume enclosed, and give me an opportunity to discuss personally with you my possible contribution potential to your Company.

Sincerely,

Thomas Hardy
(123) 456-7890

A GENERAL LETTER INTRODUCING A RÉSUMÉ

Frederick Ochs
220 Park Place
Jersey City, N. J. 12345
(201) 123-9876

The Bristol Company
30 Raymond Blvd.
Newark, N. J. 07100

Att'n: Mr. Raymond Aken, Director
Personnel Administration

Gentlemen:

With 22 years of sales management and personal sales experience selling to chains, distributors, department stores, and a demonstrated ability to increase sales by substantial amounts with a high sense of profit responsibility, I am qualified for a management position with your Company.

My resume is enclosed. When you have reviewed it, the opportunity for a personal interview would be appreciated.

Sincerely yours,

FO   Frederick Ochs

LETTER WRITTEN BY AN INTERMEDIARY
ON BEHALF OF A JOB APPLICANT

The XYZ Corporation
666 Springfield Avenue
Westfield, N. J. 07901

Mr. John Q. Adams
Vice President, Marketing
Executive Vitamin Co., Inc.
300 Pennsylvania Avenue
Durham, N. C. 12345

Dear Mr. Adams:

You can employ this man whose career highlights are described on the attached page for effective contributory work in sales management in the fields of pharmaceuticals, proprietary drugs, cosmetics, appliances, accessories.

We have researched his references and they are without exception excellent.

There is no obligation to this Company in connection with his employment by you.

If you are seeking an M. B. A. with related business experience you can save search, advertising or other fees by interviewing this man who is available for immediate employment. He is willing to relocate for a good opportunity.

You may phone him direct at (123) 567-0987 to set up an interview, or you may write to him at the above address.

Sincerely,

JM/ds   Andrew Jackson

A COVERING LETTER FOR A WEAK RÉSUMÉ

Robert Hope
21271 Hermosa Street
Hermosa Beach, California 10000
(321) 098-7654

Dear Sir:

I have been attending Cal-Tech since 1971, evenings, and most recently full time, to gain a B. E. degree in Chemical Engineering which I have just been awarded.

Engineering has been my vocational objective for many years, particularly Process Design and Development, chemically related, or Chemical Engineering. I believe I am now qualified to make positive contributions in these areas for any corporation, particularly since I have had previous administrative experience and a career in the U. S. Army which will enable me to adapt easily to responsible assignments.

The training in Engineering has been both rigorous and enjoyable and I look forward to utilizing the knowledge I have acquired in a productive way.

My resume is enclosed. May I have an interview to establish my credentials?

I look forward to your reply.

                                              Sincerely,

RH   Robert Hope

A COVERING LETTER FOR MAILING RÉSUMÉS
TO EXECUTIVE SEARCH FIRMS

Patrick Henry
100 Old Post Road
Boston, Massachusetts 02108
(617) 789-0987

Gentlemen:

I am currently employed and have enjoyed a career of sub-stantial success as a Sales Manager for a $20 million division of a large corporation.

My situation has been somewhat unique in that I have had almost autonomous responsibility in operations.

My income is in the middle 30s with comprehensive fringe benefits. I am willing to relocate for any good opportunity.

My resume is enclosed.

If you have a search in progress for someone of my qualifi-cations, I would like to explore mutual interests with you at a personal meeting.

Sincerely,

PH   Patrick Henry

Note that the covering letter mentions the salary desired. Executive search firms must know, sooner or later, a job applicant's suitability for their clients.

LETTER FOR A BROADCAST RÉSUMÉ

LAWRENCE OLIVER
20 Front Street
Portland, Me. (zip)

Dear Sir:

Employing a qualified executive at any time is
akin to having invested in IBM 20 years ago.

I have unique qualifications with a solid record
of high R.O.I. with every company I have worked
for.

The first page of the attached tells my general
story. If interested, turn to the succeeding pages
for chapter and verse.

I'd enjoy discussing with you the possibility of
being contributory to your Company. Please let
me know when I may set up an appointment with
you.

                                    Sincerely,

LO   Lawrence Oliver

A LETTER INDICATING PHYSICAL DISABILITY

William Tilden
Ropewalk Lane
Oldwick, N. J. 07000

Dear Sir:

I have a 15 year record of success in leading the R.
& D. Department (as Corporate Vice President) of a
major consumer products company which leans heavily
on expertise in electronics and mechanical engineering.

I have made many contributions to new art (for which
I am co-patentor) and have developed products which
are the leading products in my industry as you will see
from my resume, enclosed.

I am looking for broader horizons and it is possible
that my abilities would be of interest to your Company.
May we discuss it?

When I visit you, you will observe that I walk slowly
due to a broken hip which has not set properly, sus-
tained in an automobile accident. This has no effect
on my productivity.

Your reply setting up a date for a personal meeting will
be appreciated.

Sincerely,

WT   William Tilden
                                    (201) 123-5678

A LETTER UTILIZING SPECIAL LETTERHEAD DESIGN

JOHN J. DOE

1234 Kings Highway
Brooklyn, N. Y. 12345
(Home) (212) 123-4567
(Office) (212) 321-7654

Gentlemen:

With more than eleven years of successful technical and managerial experience in data processing, possessing the capability to utilize the advanced techniques available and with a record of effective leadership in the field, I am qualified to direct the Data Processing Department of any large corporation.

I am particularly interested in an association with your Company.

I have enclosed my resume, and if you have interest, the opportunity for a personal interview would be appreciated. I look forward to your reply.

                                        Sincerely,

                                        John J. Doe

JJD

LETTER TO CORPORATE EXECUTIVES,
MEMBERS OF BOARDS OF DIRECTORS, BANKERS,
AND ACCOUNTING FIRMS

100 Petticoat Lane
Far Hills, N. J. 07100

Mr. Hamilton Beach, Chairman
Bankers Holding Company
100 Wall Street
New York, N. Y. 10001

Dear Sir:

From time to time some of your larger customers,
clients or friends may ask you if you know of an
available, competent executive to guide a corporation effectively.

On the possibility that you have or may have such
a request, I am enclosing my resume which describes
a successful, contributory career.

I shall appreciate your referring to me to any opportunities which may come to your notice; or passing
this along to someone else who might have interest.

Sincerely,

ER   Edward Rickels
Encl.   (201) 321-7654

**LETTER FROM A RECENT COLLEGE GRADUATE
FOR A BROADCAST RÉSUMÉ
DIRECTED TO A SPECIFIC EMPLOYMENT AREA**

THOMAS JEFFERSON, IV
Monticello, Va. 10000

Dear Sir:

I have just graduated from the University of Maine
with a B.S. in Architectural Engineering and some
practical experience in remodeling university buildings and in some small new construction.

I hope to become associated with a Boston architectural firm.

My resume is enclosed.

May I have an appointment to discuss my qualifications with you?

I look forward to your reply.

Sincerely,

Thomas Jefferson, IV
(123) 456-7890

A GENERAL COVERING LETTER

Lewis Carroll
57 Mirror Road
Denvér, Colo. (zip)
(123) 456-7890

Mr. Henry Gladstone, Pres.
Senator Playing Card Co.
30 Mosswood Avenue
New Orleans, La.

Dear Sir:

I have a consistent record of profit contributions
arising from competence in general management,
marketing and production for major companies in
the U.S., and overseas; accustomed to P. & L.
responsibility.

I am widely experienced in power tools and sophisticated machinery.   My resume is enclosed.

May I discuss mutual opportunities in your Company
with you?

Your reply will be appreciated.

Sincerely yours,

LC   Lewis Carroll

LAYOUT OF A COVERING LETTER

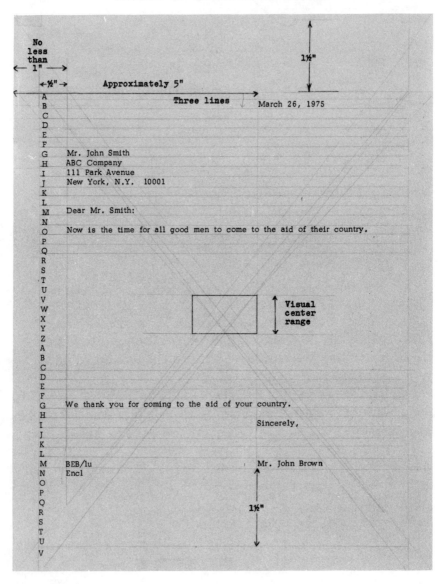

Using Your Résumé

You can make use of your résumé in a number of ways:

1. Use your résumé to answer suitable advertisements in newspapers, trade magazines, and wherever else help wanted advertisements appear.
2. Distribute the résumé among friends and acquaintances.
3. Send your résumé to members of boards of directors of local businesses.
4. Send your résumé to the companies for which you think you would like to work. Distribute as many as you can afford (at least 100) in this manner. Address the résumé to the personnel manager—either by name or by title.
5. Send your résumé to executive recruiters if you are seeking a middle or upper management position.
6. Have the résumé on hand when visiting employment agencies; they may want several copies.
7. Take the résumé to your banker, your insurance agent, your lawyer, your accountant, your broker.
8. Send your résumé to directors of trade associations related to your experience.
9. Supply a résumé to everyone who you think might be influential in getting you a job or, if you are employed, the job you would like to have.
10. Use the résumé as the basis for your presentation at an interview.

As a rule your résumé will be handled with confidentiality. Exceptions do occur, however. Thus in answering a blind advertisement you may unknowingly send a résumé to your own employer. The possibility of a breach of confidence must be considered when soliciting a position from a company other than your current employer. Weigh the potential dangers against the benefits. Though a breach of confidentiality can have disastrous results, it has on occasion served to make a company aware of a valuable employee's restlessness, leading to increased rewards for the employee. Labeling the résumé "Confidential" will not assure its confidentiality. A breach of confidentiality is usually caused by conditions outside your control.

Under some circumstances a broadcast letter is substituted for a résumé. The broadcast letter is discussed in the section that follows.

SECTION 27

The Broadcast Letter

The broadcast letter is a special type of employment application letter that is widely circulated to top company executives, rather than the personnel department. Its role derives from the fact that more than 80% of available jobs are never advertised and must be tracked down by mail.

When using the broadcast technique, whether for résumés or for letters, you judge the effectiveness of your mailing by the percentage of response, as would be the case with any mail order product. A response (inviting you to an interview) of 2% is fair; 15% is excellent.

Broadcasting is one of the quickest and most effective ways of finding a position. Send out at least 100 and preferably as many as 500 broadcast letters. The broadcast letter is used in such cases as the following:

1. Your career level makes it appropriate to bypass the personnel department.
2. Your talents and experience may have special appeal to a company executive.
3. Your special abilities may cause an executive to employ you now for a position that will actually become available only later.
4. Your qualifications might exactly meet the requirements for a position that the company has been unsuccessfully trying to fill for some time.
5. Your unusual qualifications may be particularly appreciated by a particular executive.
6. You might be well and favorably known at the top executive level of many companies.
7. Your qualifications might lead to an executive reorganization, making a place for you that did not exist until your letter acted as the catalyst to initiate such action.

8. Many top executives, including chief executive officers, like to be made aware of the availability of certain kinds of people.
9. Recruiting an executive by way of a broadcast letter can save a company thousands of dollars in search fees.

The use of a résumé in such cases would nullify your objective—résumés are almost automatically routed to personnel departments. Your broadcast letter might lead to requests for your résumé, which, sent at this point, serve the positive function of satisfying the company's affirmative interest in you.

By using the broadcast letter approach you are not depreciating the personnel department. Many personnel departments do not handle the employment of personnel at higher levels where the subtleties of character and required expertise are difficult to gauge. Employment ideas, amorphous at first, often may be formed only after an interview. Many corporations do not even list employment directors by name in the standard directories.

Fit your broadcast letter on one page. It is really a summary of a summary. It is easier to write this letter if you have a good résumé from which to extract the information.

Start the letter by identifying yourself and your field of specialization:

I have 15 years of successful, progressive experience in marketing management in the pharmaceutical and health care fields with an $100 million company.

State your objective:

I want to become associated with a medium size company or a division of a large company in the Southwest or Midwest where I will have complete marketing responsibility and opportunity for growth to general management.

List some of your accomplishments:

In six years I increased regional sales of pharmaceutical and health care products from $9 million to more than $30 million while maintaining or improving profitability.

Recruited, trained, and led a sales force of 60 salesmen, 3 field assistants and 7 district managers.

Three of the 7 district managers under my leadership were awarded "Manager of the Year" recognition.

Indicate special qualities:

I have been a successful salesman. I have trained scores of salesmen and managers to sell and manage effectively. I am innovative, motivated, and dedicated and possess the quality of leadership to a degree that has made my region first among all company regions in four of the last seven years. I am experienced in budgeting, forecasting, advertising, promotion, and compensation administration.

Give favorable statistics:

M.B.A.; B.A. in marketing; age 35; married.

Ask for an answer:

I would like a personal interview to discuss my potential for contributing to your company and opportunities for me to grow within your company. I look forward to your reply.

Broadcast letters may take up too much of the page to leave room for a full heading (name and address). To personalize them, use the salutation only, such as "Dear Mr. Jones."

Examples of broadcast letters follow. One broadcast letter similar to those shown produced an unprecented response of 75%, a significant number of which suggested interviews or left the way open for later follow-up.

BROADCAST LETTER FROM AN R&D EXECUTIVE

Dear Sir:

Can you utilize my abilities? For fifteen years I have been successful and innovative for a multi-million dollar company as Manager of Research and Development in the consumer products field.

My general assignment is to provide my Company with a continuing and timely
supply of new designs and competitively superior products relating to all aspects
of development of mechanical and electrical consumer products.

In carrying out my assignment, I have advanced consistently through the organization to increasing responsibilities starting as Project Engineer and successively as
Chief Development Engineer, Development Manager, Project Manager to present
position.

My accomplishments include:

- Design and development leadership in creating famous product now marketed internationally.

- Cost reduction projects that saved Company millions of dollars and resulted in
  the revitalized marketing of established products with a substantial contribution
  to corporate volume.

- Patents involving new art.

- A new approach to research and development evaluation procedures providing full
  performance functioning not before available and contributing both to better product and to improved customer relations.

- Consistent operation within budget and for 1974 a budget saving of $\frac{1}{2}$ million
  dollars, while maintaining full and effective services.

My experience includes management and leadership of large technical groups, technical writing, product evaluation procedures, project programming, budget administration, computerization of data and primarily the exercise of pragmatic creativity
in the approach to successful product development.

Hold B. S. and M. S. degrees in Engineering. Age 53, married, three children,
own home, excellent health.

                                        Sincerely,

BROADCAST LETTER FROM AN
INTERNATIONAL MARKETING EXECUTIVE

Dear Sir:

My background is ten years of intensive training and successful administration in marketing a wide range of consumer products including major appliances in South America with profit-center responsibility for $22 to $36 million operations for a multi-billion dollar international corporation.

- In 1974 I made a profit study which led to the discontinuance of unprofitable operations and a saving of $1 million annually in G. & A. expenses.

- In 1973 I established a new dealer structure and introduced six new products recommended by me which added over a million dollars to annual volume.

- From 1970 to 1973 I increased sales with another group of new products from $50,000 to $1 million.

- In 1968-1969 as a retail store manager, I increased sales from $400,000 to $600,000.

I have successfully trained hundreds of sales managers and salesmen. I am experienced in budgeting, sales forecasting, market research, advertising, product analysis. I have a strong profit motivation and have demonstrated high leadership qualities.

Age 33, married, excellent health, B. S., Accounting, fluent in Portuguese, Spanish and French.

May I have an interview to discuss my potential contributions to your Company?

I look forward to your reply.

                                        Sincerely,

BROADCAST LETTER FROM A MARKETING EXECUTIVE

Dear Sir:

I am seeking to associate with a medium size company or a division of a large company in the Southwest where I will have complete marketing autonomy with senior general management opportunity.

I am accustomed to multi-million dollar marketing responsibilities for corporations in the office equipment industry.

My current responsibility is Marketing Development for Smith & Company, Inc., known world-wide for management excellence.

The following might indicate my potential for you:

- increased Company's revenues in the Eastern Region by 53% in three years by identification of new markets and new applications for existing products.

- headed marketing team in the analysis of a new market and its requirements leading to the development of a new multi-million dollar market.

- created complete marketing plan for these new products.

- learned basic selling in door-to-door canvassing on a commission basis for leading manufacturer of photocopiers after earning M. B. A.

I am thoroughly indoctrinated with advanced marketing and management techniques; have received company awards for outstanding contributions; believe that I can make significant profitability and management contributions to a company in the consumer products area.

Age 35, married, excellent health. Undergraduate degree in Economics; Dean's List; Honor Roll; graduated in top 10% of class.

If my qualifications are of interest, I would like to have a personal interview.

I look forward with great interest to hearing from you.

                                        Sincerely,

BROADCAST LETTER FROM A GENERAL EXECUTIVE

Dear Sir:

Your investment in the creative mind of an experienced executive can produce greater returns in the next 15 years than almost any other you can make.

I am such an executive. You may be interested in a man competent in Corporate Planning and Economic Development. Here are some of my accomplishments:

- As a negotiator represented an aircraft company for contracts involving over $50,000,000 in sales. I am skilled in management and government agency interface, verbally and in writing.

- As an aerospace engineer I was among the first to introduce and implement Systems Engineering Management procedures. I am familiar with the important methods of profitability management; management by objective, management by exception, PERT and other

- As C. E. O. of a company, I developed programs to assist economic development in the Caribbean through use of Systems Management in accomplishing industrial breakthroughs.

I have a record of adding $100 million in extra profits to three companies by whom I have been employed.

Age 50, married, three children, excellent health, B. A., Economics.

Can you use an Executive with these qualifications in your business? If you can, let's discuss it. I'd like to work for you.

Your reply will be appreciated.

Sincerely,

BROADCAST LETTER FROM A SALES EXECUTIVE

Dear Sir:

I am 35 years old, well educated, motivated, with successful experience in sales, office management, PR/client relations and advertising. I am currently employed with a national temporary employment organization in a management capacity.

I seek a position that provides opportunity for growth to management preferably in a people-oriented environment where I can utilize abilities in persuasion, communications and leadership such as: sales promotion, PR, communications, advertising, film production; willing to travel.

Some of my achievements:

- increased business $100% for present employer by selling services to new accounts.

- worked with PR firm in organizing and producing successful fashion shows, obtaining talent, choosing garments, accessorizing, photography and writing including press releases.

- supplied effective help in copywriting production of sales films, scripts, story boards;and market research for major consumer goods client of well known advertising agency.

I have extensive training and experience in the performing arts under nationally known teachers; was a National Honor Student; have won State awards in writing and mathematics.

May I discuss with you my potentials for contributing to your Company while developing my own career?

I look forward to hearing from you.

Sincerely,

BROADCAST LETTER FROM A FINANCIAL EXECUTIVE

Dear Sir:

I have 15 years of successful experience in financial areas: six years as bond analyst for a leading underwriter; six years as editor, writer and analyst for a large investment advisory service; three years as a research analyst for a major Boston bank.

My competence includes the ability to make effective underwriting presentations to achieve better bond ratings through restructured analyses, understanding of legal requirements in connection with, and effectiveness in, accomplishing sales closings.

I am accustomed to the orderly presentation of complex financial and economic data, the preparation and finalization of all official statements and have a complete understanding of money and capital markets and exchanges. I am also familiar with and experienced in regional specialization, and have an excellent knowledge of marketing techniques.

I would like a personal interview to discuss with you how I might be contributory to your organization while furthering my own career.

My educational background includes M. B. A. and B. S. degrees in finance. Personal data: age 36, married, excellent health, prefer Boston location.

Your response will be appreciated.

                                                              Sincerely,

BROADCAST LETTER FROM A MARKETING EXECUTIVE

Gentlemen:

With 15 years of successful experience in marketing management for
major companies largely involving power tools and a record of consistent progress from salesman to manager of a $30 million region,
I am a qualified marketing executive.

Among my accomplishments:

- over a period of six years increased regional sales from $9 million
  to nearly $30 million while staying well within profitability guide-
  lines.
- recruited, trained and led a sales force of 60 salesmen with two
  field assistants and seven district managers.
- of seven district managers under my leadership, two ranked first
  and second nationally with the first awarded recognition as <u>Manager
  of the Year</u>.
- planned effective promotions and advertising on the way to achieving sales increases described.
- successfully promoted 25 of my salesmen into corporate positions
  in various areas: Product Planning, Marketing, Regional and District
  Management.
- upon assignment to important Atlanta District brought it from fifth
  to first place in sales and earnings and won <u>Manager of the Year</u>
  Award.
- earlier developed District which ranked last in sales to fourth position nationally.
- as salesman was routinely among top salesmen in the U. S., win-
  ning sales contests and earning numerous awards.

I am an effective innovator, sales leader and trainer, with a solid
background in modern management techniques and concepts, banking
and finance. B. S., Business Administration, age 40, married, two
children, own home, excellent health.

I seek a position as Director of Marketing or General Sales Manager
for a medium size corporation in the tool industry.

If my qualifications are of interest to you, I would like an opportunity
for a personal meeting.

                                        Sincerely,

SECTION 28

Mailing Lists

The names and addresses of corporations and organizations and the names of their personnel can be obtained from the following sources found in most libraries:

1. Dun and Bradstreet *Reference Book of Corporate Management*.
2. Telephone directory Yellow Pages (company and organization names and addresses only).
3. Standard and Poor's Register of Corporations, Directors, and Executives.
4. State industrial directories.
5. Industry associations (almost all major industry classifications have one).
6. Thomas' Register of American Manufacturers.
7. Martindale-Hubbell Law Directory.
8. Moody's Handbook of Common Stocks.
9. The Value Line Investment Survey (published by Arnold Bernhard & Co., Inc.).
10. Rand McNally Bankers International Directory.
11. Fortune's annual supplement listing the 500 largest corporations (no individual executive names) and other listings.
12. Forbes annual list of 2500 corporations (no individual executive names).
13. Hardware Age Directory (published by Chilton Co., Radnor, Pa.).
14. Pharmaceutical Handbook.
15. Other trade magazines.
16. The Standard Advertising Register.
17. American Management Association publications (such as Executive Search Firms).
18. The Literary Marketplace.
19. Standard Rate and Data Service.
20. United States Government Organization Manual.
21. Directory of Foundations in Massachusetts.
22. College Placement Annuals.
23. Association of Consulting Management Engineers (New York City).
24. The Wall Street Journal daily list of corporate operating reports.

Such publications as Dun and Bradstreet and Standard and Poor's give the S.I.C. (Standard Industrial Classification) numbers, which permit you to select companies in specific industrial areas.

Corporate and personnel changes are taking place constantly. No directory can be completely up-to-date. Some of the individuals listed in a directory will have retired, died, resigned, or been fired since its publication. To avoid misdirecting your letters, purchase a rubber stamp reading "Attn: Executive Secretary. If addressee is incorrect please route to proper individual" for use on all letters addressed to individuals by name. If using the name of a person is very important, telephone the company or organization for the information.

A P P E N D I X   A
Supplementary Résumé Examples

In this appendix we reproduce 20 résumés, in addition to the 37 résumés scattered throughout the book. To find the résumé you want, consult the Index of Résumés at the end of the book.

RÉSUMÉ OF A FASHION INDUSTRY LEADER

3040 River View   (914) 123-4567
Hastings-on-Hudson, N. Y. 10021

R E S U M E

of

ANNE MARIE TODD

qualified as

FASHION/FABRIC EDITOR

or for

FASHION-RELATED POSITION IN ADVERTISING, PUBLIC RELATIONS

---

* * *   Recognized authority and analyst in fashion and fabrics, for men and women with ability to write, lecture, train; imaginative in coordinating fashion elements; technical fabric knowledge; excellent trade relationships.

* * *   Experienced in large segment of fashion industry, in merchandising and promotion, store operations, fashion shows, public relations, organizing, editing. Familiar with home sewing and craft industries. Accept responsibility and execute. Trained in budget preparation and presentation.

* * *   Eighteen years as successful associate editor, fabric editor, promoter, trend forecaster, for three of the most important magazines in the field of fashion.

* * *   Made patterns and crafts segments of one magazine so attractive to readers that pattern pages were doubled and crafts pages increased four-fold.

* * *   Consistent record of career development in fashion industry.

FOR FURTHER DATA PLEASE SEE FOLLOWING PAGES

ANNE MARIE TODD   PAGE 2

BUSINESS EXPERIENCE:

1972-Present   SYNTHETIC YARN ASSOCIATION, New York, N. Y.

DIRECTOR of promotional unit of synthetics industry representing about 90% of
all U. S. Producers, including all major mills. Report to Board of Directors
of Council. Responsible for:

- publicity, merchandising, promotion, using all communications media in all
  markets for Men's, Women's and Children's Fashions.

Accomplishments:

- Put together and stage fashion shows for TV across the country and arrange
  publicity tying in with leading department stores; acclaimed by manufacturers, designers, retailers and public for excellence; strong press coverage,
  radio interviews.

- conduct important fashion show annually, including Men's Wear; attended
  by more than 1,000.

- prepare and present budgets for board approval on monthly basis; make
  quarterly presentations to industry.

1969-1972   VOGUE-BAZAAR MAGAZINE, New York, N. Y.

Employed in Fashion Department as FABRIC EDITOR, working for Executive Editor of this internationally famous magazine directed to the 13-19 age market.
Responsible for:

- coverage of fabric and fashion markets to be continuously current and ahead
  of trends in order to plan, coordinate and execute monthly fashion pages;
  study and report on color evolutions.

- conducting public relations programs, representing magazine as lecturing
  fashion authority; attend fashion shows and business conferences around
  U. S. and overseas; consult with clients with respect to outlooks, fashion
  guidance.

- autonomy to approve fashion pages in absence of Editor.

Accomplishments:

- pages devoted to fabrics doubled and tripled respectively due both to increased reader interest and better, more interesting pages.

- first Fabric Editor at magazine to be sent to Europe to cover Frankfurt
  Fair to report on European influences.

over please

ANNE MARIE TODD   PAGE 3

- made successful presentations to advertisers of such companies as Monsanto, J. P. Stevens, DuPont, Celanese.

- new promotions, such as Dior Daytime Patterns, tied in with major department and specialty stores nationally.

- responsibility for new section and magazine cover tying in with Nieman-Marcus and Post-Teen Department.

1967-1969   CITY, TOWN & COUNTRY, New York, N. Y.

ASSISTANT TO DIRECTOR OF MERCHANDISING AND PROMOTION with responsibility for fabric and fashion promotion.

- edited and supervised production of promotional brochures including fabric reports.

- made presentations to retail buyers on importance and effectiveness of editorial pages; worked cooperative advertising programs with multi-million dollar corporations.

1956-1967   BUTTERY PATTERN COMPANY, New York, N. Y.

Successively ASSISTANT SERVICE EDITOR, ASSOCIATE EDITOR.

- as Fabric Editor, covered fabric market intensively, presented ideas and prognostications to staff, clients, buyers; acted in PR capacity.

- predicted color and design trends; maintained library; epitomized market.

Work was widely recognized resulting in unsolicited job offers from three of the major fashion magazines.

EDUCATION:

JESUIT COLLEGE, Kansas City, Mo. 1950-1954.

B. S., Merchandising.

HOBBIES:

Scuba diving, gourmet cooking, travel.

PERSONAL DATA:

Age 39, married.

REFERENCES AND FURTHER DATA ON REQUEST

RÉSUMÉ OF AN E.D.P. PROGRAMMER

13 A Avenue   (212) 213-7654

R E S U M E

of

HARLAN NYQUIST

qualified as

SYSTEMS/PROGRAMER ANALYST

---

* * *   Twelve years of comprehensive experience in Data Processing including supervision, computer systems development,
programing and operations.

* * *   Broad experience in systems design for IBM 379, 360,
1400 computer series involving all types of computer application. Fully experienced with COBOL, BAL, System-3
RPG II, autocode, IOCS and SPS programing applications.

* * *   Experience includes nearly six years as Systems Analyst
planning and collaborating with departments to coordinate
their activities with computer systems.

* * *   Designed and programed departmental systems and procedures
from conception to completion. Handled all phases of problem solving related to these applications.

* * *   Age 32, excellent health.

FOR FURTHER DETAILS PLEASE SEE FOLLOWING PAGES

EXPERIENCE:

1971-Present   MANUFACTURERS GREENWICH TRUST CO., New York, N. Y.

  1973-Present   PROJECT ANALYST for major New York bank in charge of all
                     phases of all projects assigned. Responsible for:

  - design and redesign of General Ledger System for entire bank; wrote pro-
    grams in RPG II; implemented system.
  - working in various phases of DDA system.
  - working on branch clearing system, commercial loan system utilizing OS,
    JLC, DOS, JLC RPG, OCS including programing in RPG II, BAL and COBOL.
  - writing specifications for modifications of systems and follow through pro-
    graming as supervisor up to implementation of systems.

  Trained under Morgan-Hanover program by Burroughs in Information Management
  System (IMS)

  1971-1973   TEAM MEMBER, Master Charge Credit Card Accounting Auth-
                    orization System.

  Part of a team responsible for implementing a complete on-line Master Charge
  credit card authorization system. Specific responsibilities were to design and
  write program specifications and programs to convert the merchant and card-
  holder data bases. In addition, designed test data to test the entire system,
  modified and wrote additional programs and operation procedures. This included testing and solving problems which arose. Frequently traveled out-of-state
  to work out implementation problems. System successfully completed.

  General Ledger System

  Employed as Programer/Analyst working as part of a system project team to do
  feasibility studies, design, program specification, programing, and implement a
  Manufacturers Greenwich on-line general ledger system. Responsibilities were
  data preparation and designing the on-line monitor and 10 data processing mod-
  ules. In addition, responsible for two trainee programers learning use of As-
  sembly language. Project successfully completed.

  1959-1971   GENERAL CORPORATION, New York, N. Y.

  1967-1971, employed as Programer/Analyst responsible for design of programing
  specifications and programing of General's statistical geographical advertising
  system. System completed in eight months. April, 1968, given responsibility
  to transfer the data processing operation from Los Angeles to New York. Transfer successfully completed in three months.

  Conducted feasibility study and implemented NCR 735 and 736 magnetic tapes
  encoder with communication logic to transmit data to and from six geographical
  areas of the U. S. Frequently traveled to those areas to design and implement system to reduce clerical work load.

1958-1967, IBM Wiring Technician. In one year promoted to programer; then
to Supervisor of Programing Department, supervising three trainee programers.
Designed and programed systems for payroll application (operable within six
months). Accounts Receivable, Accounts Payable, statistical statements,
sales, invoicing and other financial reports.

Converted IBM programs to S/360 DOS operation while working with various
Department Managers.

MILITARY SERVICE: U. S. ARMY, 1955-1959

Wiring Technical Specialist. Completed Army IBM Accounting Technical School.
Selected as one of six technicians to attend advance wiring system and procedure school. Assigned to train U. S. and Korean technicians to process
base inventory control data.

EDUCATION:

A. A. S., Ryder College, Trenton, N. J.

Special courses as follows:

1965-1966   COBOL Programing

1964   Introduction to IBM System 360

1962-1963   Advanced Programing: EDP System 1401

1961-1962   Programing 1401 System

Special IBM courses:

                   BRAM MACROS and Facilities
                   Introduction to System 360
                   360 COBOL
                   Advanced IOCS

                   IBM School: Basic 1401 Programing

Additional courses U. S. A. Technical School: Systems and Procedures; Advanced Wiring, Systems and Procedures; Wiring, Machine Accounting.

PERSONAL DATA:

Born December 15, 1938, excellent health.

REFERENCES AND FURTHER DATA ON REQUEST

RÉSUMÉ OF A STRUCTURAL ENGINEER

72 Erector Boulevard   (516) 300-3000
Natick, N. Y. 23456

R E S U M E

of

MALCOLM STERN

Qualified As

PROJECT ENGINEER - STRUCTURAL

Experienced, capable, innovative Structural Engineer with
record of effective participation and leadership in vitally
important and complex projects such as MOREX Building of
the (ABM) System, Kansas City Mall Power Plant Units.

Demonstrated management competence and broad engineering
comprehension by coordinating diverse engineering disciplines to effect optimum results in adhering to completion
schedules and maintaining high quality, safe design and
construction.

Excellent educational background with supporting graduate
courses in important engineering areas.

Record of remaining on job from inception to completion.
Recalled by former employers as new projects develop.

Registration: LICENSED PROFESSIONAL ENGINEER, State of
New York, No. 123456, December 1960.

B. S. Degree, age 43, married.

MALCOLM STERN   PAGE 2

EDUCATION AND ACCREDITATIONS:

B. S., Civil Engineering, Structural Option, College of Engineering, University of Denver, Denver, Colorado, 1955.

Graduate courses in Structural and Industrial Engineering, New York University, New York, New York, 1960, 1961, 1962.

Read, write, speak German, Arabic, Polish.

EXPERIENCE:

1972-Present   ELY & SIMPSON, INC., Wichita, Kansas

SENIOR STRUCTURAL ENGINEER for consulting engineering firm. Responsible for major part of review and revision of design engineering of the Library and Museum Building in the "New Kansas City" Project. Checked design of post tensioning systems coordinating with contractor on manner and sequence of systems.

1968-1972   ELY & SIMPSON, INC., New York, N. Y.

As SENIOR STRUCTURAL ENGINEER for Criteria and Design worked on:

CRITERIA

- Complex Attack Umbrella Module System (AUMC) component in conjunction with mechanical, electrical, architectural and other engineering disciplines developing design criteria and specifications for structures designed to sustain nuclear blasts. Prepared cost estimates of project components. On project from inception to completion. (Studies available for inspection).

- Specifications and design criteria for structures capable of withstanding nuclear blasts.

DESIGN

- Updating drawings to conform to latest Atlas Arms Convac interface requirements.

- Made field site visits, resolved deficiencies indicated in engineering memos.

- Supervised preparation of criteria for interdisciplinary groups.

- Maintained contact with all engineering groups, including mechanical and pipe support groups.

- Chosen to confer with A. U. M. C. Contractors and outside manufacturers' representataves.

- Remained on projects to completion.

MALCOLM STERN   PAGE 3

<u>Jan. 1968-July 1968</u>   BALL & CHAIN ENGINEERING CORP., Kew Gardens, N. Y.

As SENIOR STRUCTURAL DESIGNER:

- Supervised preparation of design drawings and reviewed industrial structures in
  steel mill plant (Italy) and gas processing furnace (Kuwait).

<u>1964-1967</u>   SENIOR STRUCTURAL DESIGNER employed through job shops
for design, coordination of other engineering disciplines, and supervision of drawings for the following firms:

- <u>U. S. Electric Power</u>, West Point, N. Y.: floor systems and air intake enclosure
  ducts of Cape Horn thermal power plant.

- <u>Maywood Corporation</u>, Hopwell, N. C.: design of compressor building, foundations, superstructures, coordinating with other engineering disciplines to completion of project.

- <u>Pasco Corporation</u>, New York, N. Y.: copper processing plants (Peru). Designed
  complete building in processing system from foundation to superstructure; remained
  on job to completion of project.

<u>1963-1964</u>   BALL & CHAIN ENGINEERING CORP., Smithtown, N. Y.

As SENIOR STRUCTURAL DESIGNER in charge of:

- design and layout of reinforced concrete underground coal handling structures and
  equipment for two 1000 MKW units, Wheelock Power, Pa., project for Florida
  Electric and Power Company.

- design, layout, checking and supervising drawings of 500 KV substation switch-
  yard, structural steel framing, on project for Charlestown Electric Power Company.

- complete superstructure and foundation – transmission towers for 500 KV switch-
  yard on Denver Power Project.

Remained on all projects to successful completion.

<u>1961-1963</u>   MAKAIGH & FINCH, New York, N. Y.

As STRUCTURAL DESIGNER participated in design of high-rise commercial and institutional buildings such as: Columbia Medical School, Church of the Holy Virgin,
Settlement, N. Y.; Pownall College buildings; B'Nai Brith Congregation, Pittsburgh,
Pa.; Foley Square Arena, New York, N. Y.; participated in stress and stability in-
vestigation and preparation of a report on Kansas City Civic Center.

<u>1959-1961</u>   ELY & SIMPSON, INC., New York, N. Y.

As STRUCTURAL ENGINEER participated in design of Terminal Building, Kennedy

MALCOLM STERN   PAGE 4

International Airport, New York, N. Y., and approach viaducts. Designed floors
and columns. Prepared complete pilot analysis and design of prototype concrete
bent of viaduct fronting terminal; design used as guide for design of other bents.

<u>1958-1959</u>   ARCO CONSTRUCTION COMPANY, Somaliland

ASSISTANT FIELD (CIVIL) ENGINEER for construction of underground reinforced concrete hangars for Somali Air Force. Supervised preparation of concrete mixes,
earth removal, road beds, paving.

<u>1957</u>   DIANA STEEL COMPANY, Jupiter, Pa.

STRUCTURAL DESIGNER working in structural steel detailing. Member of team of
seven structural engineers training in preparation for management of consulting engineering business in Israel.

<u>1956</u>   SUSS, INC., New York, N. Y.

STRUCTURAL DESIGNER. Designed various steel and reinforced concrete structures
on a Chemical Processing Plant project for Zinc plant.

<u>1955</u>   CHRYSLER ASSOCIATES, Chicago, Ill.

Worked as CIVIL ENGINEER in design, layout, drafting of municipal projects involving highway drainage, sewer and water services.

<u>PERSONAL DATA</u>:

Born 3/31/32, married, six children, own home and car. U. S. citizen.

Defense Department Security Clearance: SECRET.

Traveled extensively in Europe and Africa.

Member of American Steel and Aggregate Association.

<u>REFERENCES AND FURTHER DATA ON REQUEST</u>

RÉSUMÉ OF A DISTRIBUTION OR TRANSPORTATION EXECUTIVE

800 Moor Drive   Home: (201) 123-4567
Convent, N.J. (zip)   Office: (212) 654-3210

RESUME

of

BEN JONSON

DISTRIBUTION/TRANSPORTATION EXECUTIVE

***   Record of profit contributions in millions of dollars to two
employers in 15 years through transportation cost savings
and efficiencies arising from wide experience and continuing studies of transportation administration.

***   Qualified for executive management of corporate operations
involving personnel, facilities, equipment, procedures, inventory control and policies. Strong experience in using
computer technology to establish programs and arrive at
answers to complex problems including inventory control
and better turnover to generate improved cash flow.

***   Experienced in organization structure, manpower develop-
ment, space analysis and layout including sophisticated
warehouse planning. Demonstrated leadership qualities.

***   Experienced conference, association, seminar speaker,
negotiator with government commissions and all major rate
bureaus.

(FOR FURTHER DATA, PLEASE SEE FOLLOWING PAGES)

BEN JONSON   PAGE 2

RECORD OF EMPLOYMENT

January 1965-Present   ESBEE QUALITY PRODUCTS CO., INC., Boonton, N. J.

MANAGER, TRANSPORTATION of $250 million Company with 1000 direct-to-dealer
salesmen calling nationally on retail stores. Staff of 15 including Analysts,
Routing, Passenger, Travel, Private Transportation Supervisors, Automobile Fleet
Coordinator, Transportation Clerks.

Responsible for:

- direction and coordination of all transportation functions including recommendations of policies and procedures.
- coordination of established programs and procedures.
- providing direction to Branches and Manufacturing Units in establishing and
  maintaining adequate and efficient transportation services.
- all transportation costs and expenditures.
- administration of leasing of 1,250 automobiles for salesmen and executive staff
  and 250 delivery trucks.
- personnel travel and hotel accomodations.

In execution of responsibilities:

- issued Transportation Department Manual, Delivery Service Manual, Guide Lines
  for Transportation Profit.
- assisted all units by counseling during periodic visits.
- participated in selection of Transportation personnel.
- maintained and communicated data in connection with newest development in
  transportation.

Accomplishments include:

- development of expanded own carriage program with a 1974 saving of $318,000.
- trucking cost savings: 1972, $100,000; 1973, $200,000; 1974, $400,000.
- utilization of Air Freight Forwarding for a $300,000 saving in first year.
- substitution of an automobile lease program for automobile allowance program
  reducing salesmen's out-of-pocket expenses and saving Corporation $100,000
  annually.
- establishment of LCL and Truckload Commodity Rates to eliminate premium rates
  on mixed shipments resulting in annual corporate savings of $400,000 (prior to
  expansion of own carriage program).
- setting up additional consolidation terminal in Omaha supplementing N. J. terminal. Created transportation savings of $250,000 annually.
- by computer program eliminated scales, UPS and postage meters and operators
  in 12 branches. Saved $175,000 annually.
- developed Unitized Shipping Plan in-bound from Vendors. Expanded plan to include out-bound shipments to branches. Annual saving of $600,000.

BEN JONSON   PAGE 3

<u>1958-1965</u>   ALLIED STORES, INC., New York, N. Y.

GENERAL TRAFFIC MANAGER for $1 billion plus chain of 100 leading department
stores, supervising department of 85 people.

Accomplishments included:

- reduction of staff from 85 to 70 with annual saving of $150,000.
- development of Company Vendor Routing Guide.
- reduction in number of Shipper Association Memberships.
- improvement of shipping time to West Coast.
- increase in claims recoveries of $250,000.
- establishment of New York warehouse to handle imports.
- computer program to control imports. Reduced pier handling time by seven
  days per shipment.

<u>1953-1958</u>   PROPANE GAS COMPANY, Indianapolis, Ind.

Tank Car Supervisor, Rate Clerk, Transportation Clerk.

<u>EDUCATION</u>:

<u>B. A.</u>, University of Indiana, Indianapolis, Ind. Major, Business; Minor,
Transportation. Attended evening classes.

<u>SPECIAL SEMINARS</u>:

Attended advanced seminars in Transportation 1960-1970, evening classes.

The Management Grid, Scientific Methods, Inc., Washington, D. C.

<u>COMMUNITY PARTICIPATION</u>:

Chairman, Community Chest, three years. Citizen-of-the-Year Award.

<u>MEMBERSHIPS</u>:

President, The National Shippers Association
Board of Directors, Carrier Conference of BNT.
American Traffic Club

<u>HOBBIES</u>:

Chess, bridge, golf.

<u>PERSONAL DATA</u>:

Born 7/27/36, married, 2 children, excellent health. Willing to relocate.

<u>REFERENCES AND FURTHER DATA ON REQUEST</u>

RÉSUMÉ OF A MANAGEMENT CONSULTANT

44 Lincoln Avenue   (914) WE 9-5835
Harrison, New York   10573

VITA

<u>JOHN WILSON EDWARDS</u>

<u>CONSULTANT</u>

***   Possess creativity and ability to develop complete concepts, work out the details of implementation. Author of uniquely successful sales programs.

***   Strong record of corporate accomplishments in creating profit, maintaining profitability, training associates, achieving continuous volume increases; expert in corporate organization and remuneration plans.

***   Talented in product development as well as harmonious leadership of engineers and technical people. Able to delegate authority, give autonomy of operation where deserved.

***   Writer, author, community worker and leader, active sports participant, nationally known and respected in his industry, able to envisage great designs and bring them to fruition.

***   Widely traveled throughout the U.S. and in Europe, with an excellent educational background in the Arts, Finance and Law.

JOHN WILSON EDWARDS   Page 2

<u>1965-Present</u>   EDWARDS & HAZLETT, INC., 32 W. 42nd St., N.Y.C.

PRESIDENT of consulting firm specializing in management, marketing and advertising. PRESIDENT of subsidiary company, specializing in corporate recruiting, career planning for individuals.

<u>1940-1965</u>   J. JOHNSON & CO., 37 Roark St., Nashville, Tenn.

FIRST VICE PRESIDENT, DIRECTOR, only non-family Officer and Director of family-owned cutlery manufacturing company, largest in its field, with international distribution, annual volume of $30 million.

Sales made to more than 40 kinds of industrial distributors, hardware wholesalers, department stores, mass merchandisers, national and regional chains, catalog and premium companies, notions wholesalers, garden and seed companies, florists, governments, sheet metal companies, gift wholesalers.

Elected VICE PRESIDENT in 1955 and responsible for:

- Sales - domestic and foreign.
- National consumer, trade, institutional advertising, catalogues, circulars, displays, packaging.
- Public relations.
- Marketing budgets and forecasting.
- Market research.
- Terms of sale.
- Production control statistics.
- Marketing department remuneration.
- Mergers and acquisitions.
- Company representation at major trade and business functions, receptions.
- Legal liaison.
- Product research and development.
- Warehousing and Shipping.
- Profitability with President and Treasurer.

During this period, sales increased at an annual rate of 10% <u>without benefit of new products</u>.

These things were accomplished:

- 72% of the market for one group of products representing approximately 50% of company's total sales.

- 55% of the market for another product group representing 25% of company sales.

JOHN WILSON EDWARDS   Page 3

- 25% of the market for a third classification of company business in competition with such giants as Allegheny-Ludlum, Stanley, Ames, and a multitute of smaller manufacturers.

- Complete domination of the department store market with 97% distribution accomplished among major and medium sized stores. Balance of department store distribution accomplished through wholesalers.

- Representation in every major national catalogue.

- Recognized leadership in a national program of trade education.

- Consistently high magazine readership ratings by professional rating companies.

- Acquisition of a related cutlery manufacturing company for a price equal to the value of the land alone two years after acquisition.

- A direct selling cost (salesmen's salaries, commissions and travel expenses) of 3.2%.

- A new system of computer reporting that provided a complete reading of the company position, sales, sales vs. forecast, production, production vs. goal, and profit, weekly (application of all general systems theory).

- Personally redesigned several garden products to meet or nullify competitive products of giant competitors.

- Establishment of accurate pricing formula with timely utilizations to assure a continuing profit level substantially above competitors and significantly better than most corporations in the United States.

- Establishment of brand name known to millions of consumers to a degree far exceeding the norm for a company of its size and budget.

- Effective Robinson-Patman compliance while still maintaining competitive advantages.

- Awards from trade magazines and trade associations for preeminent excellence in merchandising, policy, advertising, packaging.

<u>1950-1955</u>   SAME COMPANY AS ABOVE

SALES AND ADVERTISING MANAGER. Responsible for complete marketing of company's products.

While acting in the above capacity, responsible for:

- Designing a sales presentation for department stores successful in placing line with almost every major store in the U. S. and many in Europe.

- Creating a program for hardware wholesalers resulting in the highest accumulation of orders ever taken in the cutlery industry before or since for a single campaign and leading to almost unanimous acceptance of product line by wholesalers nationally.

- Recognition of dealer-owned groups as an important influence in hardware distribution and among the first to sell them despite objection of full-function wholesalers.

- Establishment of company products in new outlets resulting in millions of dollars annually.

- Molding of a sales force so responsive that almost any hardware or department store product of merit could have been added to the line with assurance of sales success.

- Added to the line after ten years of persuasion a product made by others and increasingly popular. Once added, within five years, company had gained 75% of total market.

- Marketing a product which had been unsuccessful for 7 years and making it into a product so successful that it finally represented 19% of total volume. Maintained dominance for product despite cheap competitive copies at 15% of the company price.

- Press parties for magazine and newspaper distributors and staffs which gained hundreds of thousands of dollars of free publicity and launched company to new sales heights.

- Starting sales planning that enabled company to grow ten times in a period of five years.

- Developed company from direct dealer selling to selling through wholesalers.

1945-1950   SAME COMPANY AS ABOVE

SALESMAN, Sales Department Assistant. Set new territory records, opened new accounts. Studied business, made proposals to Board of Directors envisioning expansion of company to double its size within five years after flat performance for preceding five years.

Gained employment contract, far exceeded established goals; increased book value of business four-fold.

EDUCATION:

B.A., St. John's College, Annapolis, Md., 1945.

L.L.B., Vanderbilt University, Nashville, Tenn., 1948. (evening attendance)

BUSINESS ASSOCIATIONS:

American Hardware Manufacturers Association - Member of Board of Directors and Executive Committee

National Idea Association - President

National Wholesalers Educational Program - Member of Committee to Design and Implement New Business Concept

State Manufacturers Association - Vice President

COMMUNITY ACTIVITIES:

Board of Directors - Community Chest

Executive Committee, Boys Club

Executive Committee - Memorial Hospital

Executive Committee - Downtown Hospital

Chairman - Community Chest State Fund-Raising Drive

Trustee - The Ethel Allen School, Avon, Connecticut

CLUBS:

Outing Golf Club, Suburban Tennis Club, Union Club, Northern Winter Club of Southern California, National Golf Club, and others.

PERSONAL DATA:

Born 4/1/26, married, three children, excellent health.

REFERENCES AND FURTHER DATA ON REQUEST

RÉSUMÉ OF A PRODUCT MANAGER

3 Bleeker Street   (212) 123-9876
New York, N. Y. 10014

R E S U M E

of

HENRY ETON

PRODUCT MANAGER

---

* * *   Evidence of considerable ingenuity in creation of
marketing plans to overcome adverse developments
successfully; to meet volume and profit targets for
product division of billion dollar conglomerate.

* * *   Consistent record of sales increases in one of the
world's most competitive and fast-moving markets.

* * *   Heavily involved in copy planning and media selection in connection with large advertising campaigns.

* * *   Expert in accommodating promotion programs to regional trade and customer characteristics; in developing
innovative packaging to enhance consumer response.

* * *   Experienced in manufacturing cost analysis and planning to restore or increase profitability. Utilizes research to adapt products to consumer preferences by
economic, geographic and other measurements.

RECORD OF EMPLOYMENT:

April 1970-Present   (Name of Company upon Request)

January 1973-Present PRODUCT MANAGER, Household Products Division, for
laundry detergent, involving interaction with staff groups, i. e., manufacturing, packaging, R. & D., legal services, sales forecasting, etc. Approximate sales of $30 million with $4 million advertising and promotion budget.

HENRY ETON   PAGE 2

Responsible for:

- marketing and profitability of detergent.

Research showed that detergent was not getting satisfactory share of market among new washer owners (to two years) although usage increased among owners of older machines (two to five years).

Developed plan for increasing use of detergent by new owners. Plan accepted by Management, implemented March 1974.

High manufacturing cost adversely affected product profit margin. Analyzed method of production.

Made recommendations to Management, accepted, resulting in increased productivity and cost saving of $250,000 annually.

1971-1972   ASSISTANT PRODUCT MANAGER, laundry detergent.

Market research indicated a potential 15% detergent loss of volume by reason of new competitive laundry detergent.

To overcome this problem, aided in development and implementation of plan involving product change, new package, revision of advertising emphasis and new promotion plan with result that detergent volume increased 20% and hit highest level in five years. Competitive product incurred severe volume loss.

1970-1971   PRODUCT MERCHANDISING ASSISTANT, hand soap.

Hand soap used discounted prices as basic customer appeal. New U. S. government regulations limited effectiveness of this approach.

Developed alternate promotion plan to comply with regulations yet maintain volume

EDUCATION:

M. B. A., Columbia University, New York, N. Y., 1974. Marketing.

B. S., St. John's University, Annapolis, Md., 1970. Business Administration.

Graduated third in class of 389. Dean's List. Listed in Who's Who Among Students in American Colleges and Universities. Awarded Key of Excellence by Society for Advancement of Management. Editor, University Newspaper.

PERSONAL DATA:

Age 26, single, excellent health, willing to relocate.

REFERENCES AND FURTHER DATA ON REQUEST

RÉSUMÉ OF PETROLEUM MARKETING EXECUTIVE

21 Central Park South   Home: (212) 123-4567
New York, N.Y. (zip)   Office: (212) 957-6543

RESUME

of

IAN FLEMING

Qualified

MARKETING EXECUTIVE in PETROLEUM/CHEMICAL INDUSTRIES

***   Widely experienced in marketing, economic and forward planning in
           petroleum and chemical industries with strong background in chem-
           istry; for large independent international oil company, and formerly
           for Getto Chemical Co.

***   Record of major contributions in increased revenues, cost savings;
           in leadership and revitalization of underproductive departments; in
           research, analysis and recommendations with respect to feedstocks,
           tankage, storage, production and marketing maximization, cost con-
           trol, economics, forecasting, budgeting.

***   Accustomed to P. & L. responsibility requiring comprehensive
           knowledge of all operations; frequently called as expert witness
           at Federal hearings affecting the petroleum industry.

***   Consistent growth with present and previous employer to positions
           of increased responsibility and excellent record of achievement in
           each position. Equipped for leadership in search for new energy
           sources and better use of energy.

***   Rhodes Scholar, First Class Honors in Chemistry. Fluent in French.

(FOR FURTHER DATA, PLEASE SEE FOLLOWING PAGES)

BUSINESS EXPERIENCE:

1969-Present   ENERGY OIL CO., New York, N.Y., $500 million
                           independent oil refiner and manufacturer of chemicals.

1972-Present, DISTRIBUTION PLANNING MANAGER. Report to V.P. Planning.
Responsible for planning and economics associated with marketing, distribution,
feedstock purchase, storage and shipping of Company products.

- developed data on costs, profit margins, availabilities permitting superior
  decision-making with risk and sensitivity evaluations.
- drew up share-of-market, distribution terminals, feedstock, optimum market,
  dockage comparison, tankage plans under normal and "energy crisis" conditions.
- act as expert witness at Government hearings on costs and prices in the oil
  industry.
- developed cost bases for increased profitability.
- thorough analysis of fuel and feedstock contracts provided basic plan for re-
  negotiations saving millions of dollars.

Result of work: raised Company margin on its petroleum and L.P.G. volume from
$6 to $8 million.

1971-1972, OPERATIONS PLANNING MANAGER, Virgin Islands. Supervised 15 graduate chemical engineers, clerical personnel. Responsible for all aspects of
planning and economics for large petroleum and petro-chemical plant including plant
utilization, costs, feedstock allocations, scheduling, storage planning, forecasting,
budgets, new plant economics.

- exercised leadership to revitalize organization and encouraged completion of
  studies on costs, tankage development and use, optimum blending, optimum
  component use, plant shut-down economics.
- from these studies made recommendations which were implemented and are now
  drawing benefits.

Asked to assume similar but increased responsibilities at N.Y. office.

1954-1965   ARABIAN CHEMICAL ET CIE, Paris, France for the French
                           affiliate of Arabian Chemical, U.S.A., largest chemical
                           company in France with revenues of $550 million, 2,700
                           employees. Company produced Ethylene, Propylene,
                           Butadiene, synthetic rubber, solvents, fuel and lubrica-
                           tion additives and specialties.

1962-1965, PLANNING GROUP MANAGER. Reported to Manufacturing Manager.
Supervised graduate engineers. Responsible for:

- feedstock evaluation.
- scheduling.
- yield monitoring.
- cost control and development.

IAN FLEMING   Page 3

- financial and production forecasts.
- economic planning.

Achievements included:

- development of department as the authoritative source of economic data and planning for the Company in France and internationally.
- saved more than $2 million annually through a mass balance/yield reporting system permitting refinement of feedstock evaluation and monitoring of plant yield deterioration at early stage.
- 4.5% reduction in utility consumption.

1960-1962, ASSISTANT MARKETING MANAGER, Paris, France. Responsible for marketing Ethylene, Propylene, Butadiene, Benzene and other industrial chemicals through contract negotiations, spot sales, development of existing customers; responsibile for profitability.

- negotiated two major contracts involving several million dollars.
- maintained and developed a series of highly profitable spot sales.
- successfully developed markets for new products.

1954-1960   HUMBLE OIL CO., Foxworth, London

1957-1960, MARKET RESEARCH. Made detailed reports on Polyolefins, oxo alcohols. Ethylene oxide and Nitriles, alcohols, plastics and world wide economic conditions. Visited Spain, England, Kuwait, Iran.

1957, LABORATORY ASSISTANT. Worked on oxidation of hydrocarbons, aromatic and aliphatic.

MILITARY SERVICE:

1952-1954   United Kingdom. Demobilized as 1st Lt./Royal Artillery.

EDUCATION:

1955-1960, Cambridge College of Technology, Cambridge, England, B.S. 1960, Associate King's Institute of Chemistry (equivalent to M.S.).

LANGUAGES:

Fluent French.

PERSONAL DATA:

Age 38, married, two children, own home, excellent health.

REFERENCES AND FURTHER DATA ON REQUEST

RÉSUMÉ INVOLVING CHANGE FROM A MILITARY CAREER

Naval Base Qtrs.
Newport News, Va. (zip)

Home: (123) 456-7890
Office: (987) 654-3210

RESUME

of

JOHN P. JONES, IV

MANAGER/EXECUTIVE
in
GENERAL ADMINISTRATION or TECHNICAL CAPACITY

***   Entire career to retirement, 1 June at age 39, with U.S. Navy with present rank of Captain. Electronics and management specialties.

***   Accustomed to command positions involving as many as 600 officers and enlisted personnel.

***   Report on fitness by commanding officers consistently either outstanding or excellent.

***   Excerpts from fitness reports include the following:

"a very dynamic officer" developing "a practical, effective and realistic organization" with "happy and well motivated subordinates"..."cost conscious".

"excellent command leadership ability, outstanding combat officer; ability to train staff in most effective use of new and experimental electronic equipment."

"excellent manager, approaches all problems in rational manner; his Section has continued to respond in a timely manner to the numerous and varied demands placed upon it and successfully pursued existing programs for equipment modernization and improved systems performance."

"demonstrated capability to handle positions of greater responsibility."

and more.

(FOR FURTHER DATA, PLEASE SEE FOLLOWING PAGES)

JOHN P. JONES IV   Page 2

EXPERIENCE:

1954-June 1975   UNITED STATES NAVY

CAPTAIN, Combat Electronics Specialty. Total of 17 assignments in Mediterra-
nean, Alaska, Bahamas, Charleston, S. C., Thailand, Washington, D. C. and
Newport News, Va. Most important assignments as follows:

Aug. 1972-June 1975, CHIEF, ELECTRONICS SCHOOL BRANCH, U. S. Navy
Training Center, Training Division. Supervise 20 officers, 93 technicians,
eight radarmen, 18 clerks. Responsible for:

- training 600 students yearly.
- establishing the curriculum.
- preparation and administration of annual budget of $2 million.

Accomplishments:

- changed curriculum, which was not relevant to needs of U. S. Navy or students, from mathematical theory to practical utilization assuring capability
  to repair electronic equipment under battle conditions.
- changed basic theory of training from one based on negative advance evaluation of students to assumption of student intelligence and positive motivation
  by description of goals.
- grades curved upwards and attrition declined from 28% to near zero.

May 1971-July 1973 , CHIEF, FACILITIES SECTION, Electronic Engineering Division, U. S. Navy Headquarters, Washington, D. C. Responsible for:

- procurement, system design and installation of all electronic equipment on
  Neptune submarines.
- justification for and preparation and administration of $500 million budget.

Accomplishments:

- issued specific job assignments to engineers by class of ship and equipment.
- discovered that surface search radar installed previously exhibited design deficiencies such as: inadequate antenna rotation, catastrophic power supply
  failures, poor video presentation, grossly inadequate mean time before failure
  (MTBF).
- increased MTBF from 16.7 hours to 260 hours within year.
- instituted program to monitor and certify all electronic installations.
- tested, developed and installed new type of transmitting antennas to better
  meet operational requirements.
- solved problem plaguing high endurance submarines for many years.

Sept. 1970-May 1971, ELECTRONICS SYSTEM DESIGNER, Cruiser Design Staff,
Electronics Engineering Division, U. S. Navy Headquarters. Responsible for:

JOHN P. JONES, IV   Page 3

   - design of communications and navigation systems with bidding specifications.

   Accomplishments:

   - new U. S. Navy Cruiser (classified) has unmatched electronic fire system ver-
     satility and complete equal air control and navigation positions.

   Sept. 1969-Sept. 1970, HIGH ENDURANCE DESTROYER SECTION, Communications
   Branch, Electronic Engineering Division, U. S. Navy Hdqtrs. Responsible for
   system design, procurement, installation of electronic equipment of 37 destroyers.

   Accomplishments:

   - developed system design for installation of new UHF, VHF/FM and VHF/AM
     communications equipment.
   - improved upon previous designs of CCTV and MF communications systems.
   - procured and installed new cameras capable of adjusting to varying light
     levels.

   Sept. 1967-Sept. 1969, SPECIAL STUDIES.

   June 1966-June 1967, COMMANDING OFFICER, U. S. Navy Command Station,
   Thailand. Supervised one officer, 28 enlisted men. Responsible for transmitting (classified) signal 99.97% each month throughout the year.

   Accomplishments:

   - transmitted usuable (classified) signal of proper power and pulse shape
     99.99% each month throughout the year.

HONORS: Bronze Star, Silver Star, Purple Heart (3), D. S. M.

EDUCATION:

   ABC Institutes, New York, N. Y., 1967-1969. Advanced Electronics Technology.
   Graduated 20th in class of 80.

   U. S. Navy Officer Candidate School, 1961 (5 months). Graduated first in class
   of 103.

   U. S. Navy Electronics School. Graduated first in class of 67.

HOBBIES: Wrestling, karate, hockey, water polo, boxing.

COMMUNITY ACTIVITIES: Coach, Scout football team.

MEMBERSHIPS: Retired Officers Association.

PERSONAL DATA: Born 6/15/36, three children, excellent health.

                    REFERENCES AND FURTHER DATA ON REQUEST

RÉSUMÉ OF A MARKETING EXECUTIVE

28 Bainbridge Place   Home: (212) 123-4567
New York, N.Y.   (zip)   Office: (212) 765-4321

RESUME

of

RICHARD STERN

Qualified As

SALES/MARKETING EXECUTIVE

***   Learned the techniques of sales management in the
field as a salesman. Developed new accounts,
opened up new territories. Handled key accounts.

***   Devised programs, displays, assortments to meet
the needs of new classes of trade. Expanded distribution. Created new selling units producing
better profits. Recruited, trained, managed salesmen.

***   Excellent contacts nationally among mass merchandisers,
chains, department stores, stamp and mail order companies, drug chains and hardware wholesalers, supermarkets.

***   Experienced in budgeting, forecasting, advertising,
sales presentations, sales meetings, remuneration,
new product development.

(FOR FURTHER DATA, PLEASE SEE FOLLOWING PAGES)

RICHARD STERN   PAGE 2

EXPERIENCE:

<u>Sept. 1969-Present</u>   (Name of Company on Request)

NATIONAL SALES MANAGER for manufacturer of household products, casters, waxes, stains, cleaners, venetian blinds, plastic covers; 200 employees and a sales force of 40 covering the entire United States. Report to President. Responsible for:

- recruiting, training and directing salesmen.

- planning participation in appropriate trade shows.

- key account development, sales and supervision.

- sales forecasts, budgets, pricing and profitability.

- new product development, displays and packaging.

- preparation of essential sales tools such as sales training material, catalog pages, advertising planning.

Successful in:

- replacing unprofitable line with highly profitable new lines, increasing volume.

- effective repackaging of entire line.

- increasing sales by means of unique and exclusive exchange plan.

- opening new accounts which added 20% to Company volume.

- developing strong accounts throughout the U. S. in areas where Company had been traditionally weak.

- meeting and outselling competitors in such accounts as Mass Merchandisers, Catalog and Mail Order Companies, Variety Chains, Drug Chains, Supermarkets.

- making Company number one in field among all above classes of trade.

Travel extensively throughout the U. S.; maintain excellent contacts with major buyers nationally.

<u>1967-1969</u>   HAMILTON CREATIONS, INC., New York, N. Y.

<u>1968-1969</u>, FIELD SALES MANAGER (Assistant to National Sales Manager) supervising sales force of 40 manufacturers representatives with department store line and separate brand for mass merchandisers.

RICHARD STERN   PAGE 3

Responsible for:

- discovering ways to increase sales.

Accomplishments:

- worked with salesmen on short trips; achieved immediate results in opening
new accounts for new department store line; appointed Field Sales Manager.

- found Company department store oriented; developed concepts for mass merchandisers to fit individual customer needs such as prearranged assortment s
using existing displays, for drug and hardware chains.

- sold hundreds of small new accounts and rack assortments without which new
line would have been dropped.

1967-1968, SALESMAN, N. Y. Metropolitan Area, for parent company and subsidiary selling consumer equipment: hampers, space savers, baskets, brush-
holders, tank cabinets, ice buckets, picnic kits, etc.

Responsible for:

- selling major department stores and independent retailers.

Accomplishments:

- created effective promotions with major accounts.

- sold new accounts including major home furnishings chain.

- increased volume over 20% in one year.

MILITARY SERVICE: U. S. Navy, 1960-1962, Boatswain's Mate First Class.

EDUCATION:

B. S., Rutgers University, New Brunswick, N. J., 1966.

HOBBIES:

Tennis, bridge, chess.

PERSONAL DATA:

Age 31, married, two children, own home, excellent health.

Willing to relocate.

REFERENCES AND FURTHER DATA ON REQUEST

RÉSUMÉ OF A FINANCIAL MARKETING EXECUTIVE

100 Pound Ridge Rd.   Home: (123) 456-7890
Clayton, Mo. (zip)   Business: (246) 321-4567

RESUME

of

JOHN T. MORRIS

Qualified In

FINANCIAL MARKETING

***

***   Strong personal motivation with successful background in management, sales,
corporate and individual financial planning, systems and organization and excellent record of volume and profit contributions in every position held from
beginning of career. Able to conceive and implement broad, complex programs to reach new goals.

***   History of numerous top awards and commendations for setting and achieving
high sales objectives as well as for developing marketing plans, motivating
staff and raising branch offices to national leadership.

***   Experienced recruiter and trainer of top producers in the industry, consistently
sought by competitive firms because of known qualities of outstanding leadership and empathy and ability to communicate.

***   Accustomed to negotiations at highest levels, assigned responsibilities for
large accounts with resulting growth and development to major status under
most competitive conditions.

***   Experienced in profit sharing, pension and insurance planning for major
corporations, and in maximum E.D.P. utilization.

(FOR FURTHER DATA, PLEASE SEE FOLLOWING PAGES)

JOHN T. MORRIS   Page 2

EXPERIENCE:

1973-Present   NEW HORIZONS RESEARCH CORP., St. Louis, Mo.

DIRECTOR of CLIENT RELATIONS for investment research company providing investment management for portfolios of individuals, pension and profit-sharing
funds, corporate accounts, trusts and institutions. Investment recommendation
featured in Forbe's (1/15/75). Responsible for:

- marketing management, marketing research, gaining new clients, liaison with
  existing clients.

Accomplishments:

- created complete marketing program where no program existed.

- trained network of Registered Representatives working for N.Y.S.E. member
  brokerage firms to sell our services.

- gained listing on Hemphill, Merrill, Hayden, Bache & Smith, Inc. approved
  list of investment advisors.

- initiated tax advisory program for professional individuals through a prominent
  Missouri law firm to assist with:

    * incorporating individuals
    * pension and profit-sharing plans
    * deferred compensation
    * Keogh plans.

- achieving letter of intent to manage $50 million in-house investment manage-
  ment program for large brokerage firm to begin in January upon expiration of
  contract with another firm.

1968-1973   CORVATH, HAYES CO., St. Louis, Mo.

MANAGER, St. Louis Office, (earlier Assistant Manager), for national brokerage
with 80 offices from coast-to-coast and total assets approaching one billion
dollars. The company handles retail, commercial and corporate accounts and
deals in preferred and common stock, corporate and municipal bonds, mutual
funds and insurance for corporations. Supervise 29 salesmen through three
Assistant Managers and back-office staff of nine. Responsible for:

- setting up new salesmen, training program, establishing guidelines for sales
  approaches, encouraging customer contacts.

- handling new stock and bond offering calendar.

JOHN T. MORRIS   Page 3

- personal selling, providing investment ideas, generating sales.
- liaison with leading corporations whose stock is recommended.
- corporate profit-sharing, pension and insurance planning for major companies.

Accomplishments:

- brought office to second most profitable nationally from a position seldom among top 20.

- recruited and trained the two top producers in the office who now rank among the top ten nationwide.

- personally generated substantial sales while concurrently effective in administrative duties.

1962-1968   CONROY ELLIMAN SECURITIES, Mission Hills, Kansas.

SALESMAN FOR BROKERAGE FIRM.

- increased personal sales production over 200% in six years.
- awarded gold prize for generating $10,000 in commissions in one month.
- awarded diamond prize for generating $20,000 in commissions in one month.
- chosen to speak to 200 salesmen on Salesmanship at headquarters meeting.
- won five-day trip to Hawaii in Mutual Funds Sales Contest.

1960-1962   MERRILL, SMITH & MORGAN, New York, N. Y.

SECURITY ANALYST, RESEARCH TRAINEE for large brokerage firm. Received excellent training for future personal development in financial selling, service and analysis.

EDUCATION:

B. S., Economics, University of Kansas, Kansas City, Kansas, 1960.

OUTSIDE ACTIVITIES:

Instructor, Adult Education Classes, N. Y. Stock Exchange program.
Coach, Youth Athletic Association baseball team.

MEMBERSHIPS: Bond Club of Missouri; Member, Chamber of Commerce

PERSONAL DATA: Born 1/31/38, married, three children, own home, excellent health.

REFERENCES AND FURTHER DATA ON REQUEST

RÉSUMÉ OF THE CHIEF EXECUTIVE OFFICER
FOR A SMALL COMPANY

Studio City   (916) 321-4567
Los Angeles, Calif. 56432

R E S U M E

of

OLIVER HARDY

CORPORATE EXECUTIVE

* * *   Exceptionally consistent record of turning loss-operated companies into viable profit-makers. Most recently, increased sales and production four times in less than three years.

* * *   Highly skilled in all phases of Management, Production, Marketing, Finance; ability to project ahead, meet and exceed goals. Able to use all most advanced management tools in administration of corporate leadership.

* * *   Expert in all metal production: forgings, stampings, castings; labor and employee relations, cost control, value analysis. Talented in product design, accustomed to R. & D. leadership.

* * *   Married, two children, B. S. Degree. Willing to relocate.

FOR FURTHER DATA PLEASE SEE FOLLOWING PAGES

OLIVER HARDY   Page 2

1968-1974   SPRING EQUIPMENT CO., New York, N.Y.

PRESIDENT, $30 million division of internationally known $350 million conglomerate.
Manufacturers of metal components for Industry and Consumer Products.

- responsible for complete administration of this Division: Marketing, Production,
  Finance.

- reorganized Division:

    * established new management structure; recruited and trained new
      executive team.

    * computerized inventory controls, order processing and invoicing.

    * eliminated losses amounting to 30% of net sales; put Division on a
      profit-producing basis; established capital expenditure budgets.

    * set up new marketing plan; hired and trained additional salesmen;
      set up cooperative advertising program; revised consumer product lines.

- multiplied sales four times in less than three years.

- personally developed new consumer product; enthusiastically accepted by
  customers.

- created five-year plan for Company, established sales goals, equipment,
  space and manpower needs, capital requirements.

- achieved sales increases in excess of 35% for 1972 and 1973 when industry
  generally was suffering a recession. (The ten year growth rate of the
  industry from 1964 was 10% compounded.)

- revised plant layout; expanded capacity; installed new equipment, liquidated
  obsolete inventories. Added key elements required to make production flow
  with speed and economy.

1960-1968   CLOVER STAMPLING CO., Rahway, N.J.

Manufacturer of tool boxes, stamped garden tools. Division of AMCO.
Successively VICE PRESIDENT, MANUFACTURING, EXECUTIVE VICE PRESIDENT,
PRESIDENT (1964-1968).

- replaced President, Vice President and Treasurer with new management team.

OLIVER HARDY   Page 3

- turned four years of losses into operation at a profit.

- set up cost reductions and strict cost controls.

- revised marketing strategy.

- made major revisions in product line.

- created new management groups for marketing and manufacturing.

<u>1953-1960</u>   A.B.C. LTD., Saskatchewan, Manitoba, Canada,
                                   $35 million manufacturer of power tools.

WORKS MANAGER in full charge of manufacturing including Industrial Engineering,
Production Control, Quality Control, Manufacturing Engineering and Product
Development:

- organized manufacturing group with clearly defined line and staff responsibilities.

- consolidated two plants with resulting cost economies.

- developed technical expertise in metal stamping, electric motors.

- expanded plant capacity by addition of own electric motor manufacturing.

- improved labor-union relations through understanding and cooperative management.

- participated in development of company to pre-eminent position in Canada and
  an important factor on the Continent.

<u>EDUCATION</u>: <u>B.S.</u>, Renselaer Polytechnic Institute, Troy, N.Y., 1948.
              Honors student. Class President; four letters in sports.

<u>MILITARY SERVICE</u>: 1940-1946, U.S. ARMY, Infantry, as Private in 1939. Attained
                    rank of Colonel in 1946.

<u>PERSONAL DATA</u>: 52 years old, married, two children. Hobbies include shooting,
                  golf. Won Swiss Pairs bridge tournament. Willing to relocate,
                  travel. Excellent health.

                    REFERENCES AND FURTHER DATA ON REQUEST

RÉSUMÉ OF A COMMUNICATIONS SPECIALIST

375 Jamaica Avenue   Home: (212) 123-4567
Forest Hills, N.Y. (zip)   Office: (212) 321-7654

RESUME

of

WILLIAM BROWN

Qualified As

COMMUNICATIONS EXECUTIVE

***   Experience in quasi-public tri-state Authority in the
         management of complex EDP and other equipment for
         the in-put, reception, storage, security and retrieval
         of vital information.

***   Record as effective manager, trainer, administrator,
         implementer in a series of demanding positions re-
         quiring specialized expertise and leadership ability.
         Top government security clearance.

***   Strong communication skills - verbal, mechanical or
         electronic - with ability to maintain any communica-
         tions system at peak performance level.

***   Earlier, similar experience in the U.S. Navy as
         Commander.

(FOR FURTHER DATA, PLEASE SEE FOLLOWING PAGES)

*   Demonstrating broad administrative, interpretative and budget skills, political
    aptitudes in exacting post with Tri-State Authority.

1970-Present   (NAME OF AUTHORITY ON REQUEST)

> ASSISTANT CHIEF OF ADMINISTRATION for Fiscal Department responsible for all
> Authority funds. Supervise staff of 50 including accountants, administrators,
> guards, clerks, etc.

*   Responsibilities and Accomplishments:

    -   act as liaison officer between Chief of Administration and all Bureau and
        Division Chiefs in the selection of personnel.
    -   administrator of payroll, attendance records and efficiency ratings of personnel.
    -   establish policy with Chief of Administration.
    -   supervise purchasing, distribution; bindery and reproduction services; custody,
        preservation and retrieval of public records; physical inventories of machines,
        furniture, files.
    -   control cash accounts for official and personnel disbursements.
    -   issue directives and procedures affecting status of employees.
    -   supervise processing of legal documents, court orders.
    -   act as Chief of Administration in absence of Chief.
    -   prepare annual estimates of the official Expense Budget.
    -   authorize, by personal signature, important financial and administrative
        documents.

*   Assigned responsibilities ordinarily accompanying rank of Captain, carried out
    assignments with distinction.

1968-1970   U.S. NAVY, U.K. COMMUNICATIONS REGION,
                                Eastbourne, Scotland

*   Responsible for:

    -   monthly inspection of maintenance equipment, for personnel and their functions
        in ten Communications Sections.
    -   coordination of training programs, installations, scheduling and administration
        of staff visits; implementation of security.

*   Initiated, developed and supervised new Maintenance Officer Evaluation Program for
    purpose of improving competence and efficiency of Maintenance Personnel.

*   Gained broad working knowledge of sophisticated wideband, microwave, multiplex
    and transospheric scatter communications systems.

1967-1968   U.S. NAVY, Bergen, Norway

> COMPUTER AUTOMATIC SWITCHING CENTER MANAGER. Supervised 50 computer
> technicians in the proper transfer of computer activity from contractor to U.S.N.

WILLIAM BROWN Page 3

* Responsible for maintenance, training and supply.
* Processed over one million messages without computer malfunction.
* Engineered program to discover computer trends. Received letter of appreciation from manufacturer.

1963-1967 U. S. NAVY, Newport News, Virginia

COMPUTER MAINTENANCE MANAGER. Responsible for:

* liaison and coordination among IBM Dayco and Navy.
* maintenance of New York "Tanker Mining Defense System" (TDMS) 1441 computer.
* all training and supply programs.
* supervision of 70 computer technicians.

* Accomplished least amount of computer down-time within U. S. Navy over three year period.

* Had coordination and maintenance responsibility for unique Acronym network Digital Data Center (DDC) transfer program. Set up training program.

* Directed over all maintenance of 360/370 computer, transmitter/receiver site and cryptographic equipment, utilized to identify and control ship traffic throughout New York Harbor. Supervised all facets of installation, inspection, repair calibration, alignment and overhaul of complex digital computer systems, establishing best Force with 55% of authorized personnel.

AFFILIATIONS:

National Automatic Data Association

Association of Communications Engineers

EDUCATION:

M. A., Education, 1965, Michigan State College, East Lansing, Mich.

B. S., Sociology, 1959, University of Toledo, Toledo, Ohio.

1961, Graduate studies in Computer Art, New York University, N. Y., N. Y.

MILITARY SCHOOLING:

Computer School, 1962-1963, U. S. N. A. Annapolis, Md., 50 weeks.
Remington-Rand Computer School, 1966-1967, 20 weeks.
Business Administration School, 1967, honor graduate.
Management Art and Science, 1968, honor graduate.

PERSONAL DATA: Born 12/31/36, married, 4 children, excellent health.

REFERENCES AND FURTHER DATA ON REQUEST

NARRATIVE RÉSUMÉ OF A PUBLIC ADMINISTRATOR

3070 Arroyo Way   Office: (123) 456-7890
San Diego, Cal.   (zip)   Home: (987) 654-3210

RESUME

of

LUIS FURPO

Qualified As

PROGRAM DIRECTOR
for
MEXICAN MIGRATORY WORKERS

EDUCATION:

    B.S., University of Mexico, Mexico City. Major: Sociology, 1960.

    M.S., University of California at Los Angeles. Major: Social Studies;
        Minor: Business Administration, 1965.

LANGUAGES:

    Fluent English, Spanish, Portuguese.

* * * * * * * * * * * * * *

Since 1966, I have been ASSISTANT DIRECTOR of the program to aid migrant workers
coming to California each year from Mexico.

My duties have been to act, pursuant to the authority of the Director, as representative of these seasonal workers in establishing a suitable work environment in areas
related to:

    Recruiting
    Housing
    Medical Care
    Transportation
    Social Adjustment

Education
Negotiation of contracts and levels of pay
Work standards and maintenance of these standards
Communication with those left at home

and to assist them in the technical aspects of:

Insurance
Entitlement under Workmen's Compensation

Specifically, I supervise a staff of 50, including two lawyers, a certified public accountant, an insurance specialist, fifteen migration specialists and three regional directors in aiding over 60,000 people each year applying to the Program for assistance and in supervising more than 20,000 agricultural workers employed on more than 1000 vineyards and farms receiving from $30 million to $40 million in payments annually.

These duties comprehend activities of the following kind:

the preparation of monthly reports with data on arrivals, departures, statistics utilizing E.D.P.

attendance at conferences, State and Federal meetings and frequently delivery of speeches at these meetings and the employer and community groups.

continuous study of State laws relating to migrant workers in every aspect of application.

visits to farms and vineyards to assure employer conformance with contracts, housing, meals, retroactive pay and the like; to conduct worker education.

In order to carry out these assignments I have studied the histories of Mexico, the U.S. and the State of California in economic, social and political terms in preparation for providing maximum assistance to Mexican workers to help them achieve full and proper participation in programs mutually established among these sovereign entities and the employers for their benefit. I also have a full knowledge of all appropriate statutes relating to contracts, insurance, workmen's compensation and of the similar work of the Puerto Rican Farm Program.

In addition, I have detailed knowledge of crops, their rotation, care and value, and of prevailing wages in the U.S. and Mexico.

This constitutes my application for the position of PROGRAM DIRECTOR, MEXICAN MIGRATORY WORKER PROGRAM, now vacant.

FURTHER DATA WILL BE FURNISHED UPON REQUEST

RÉSUMÉ OF A CONSTRUCTION EXECUTIVE

10497 Wilshire Blvd.   (123) 456-7890
Los Angeles, Cal. (zip)

RESUME

of

HARRY ZECK

*** Record of achievement in advancing to Vice Presidency of major
construction firm, after starting as supervisor of foremen.

*** Strong profit orientation with exposure in public relations,
marketing and sales; grasp of advertising strategy, direct mail
campaigns, brochures; budget planning and forecasts; successful
track record in competitive bidding situations.

*** Strength in planning new objectives, finding methods of imple-
mentation, creating millions of dollars of extra sales and profits.

*** Practical experience in project management, complete adminis-
tration of work from start to finish; payment breakdown, monthly
billing, percentage of completion, CPM or progress completion
scheduling.

*** Proven skills in field supervision, evaluation of field personnel,
labor relations, negotiations, material scheduling and expediting;
purchasing - materials and vendor subcontracts.

*** Experience in quality assurance - quality control analysis and
administration; job cost analysis, spec interpretation and
negotiating.

(FOR FURTHER DATA, PLEASE SEE FOLLOWING PAGES)

HARRY ZECK   Page 2

1965-Present   (NAME OF COMPANY ON REQUEST)

With current annual sales of $50 million, this Mechanical Contractor employs 50 office personnel and from 200 to 400 people in the field engaged in a variety of construction projects, including a recently acquired complete plant with heavy R&D investment in a patented module unit.

Scope of activities includes: piping-heating, ventilating, air conditioning; industrial piping for manufacturing, chemical, petroleum, natural gas processing; gas for turbines, instrumentation, pollution control, power generation, cryogenic facilities, cold boxes, vaporizers, barge unloading systems, liquid natural gas storage plants, vehicle loading stations for LNG service, liquid propane handling and storage systems, and alterations to existing systems.

Employed as Supervisor (1966-1969); moved up to Senior Supervisor (1969-1970) and on to Assistant Manager (1970-1971). Since then have successfully met challenges in the following succession:

* Chief Project Manager

* Assistant to V.P. Marketing

* Assistant to Executive Vice President

* Vice President Marketing Services

* Specific Achievements:

As Assistant Manager:

- developed new and better methods for estimating both HVAC and power piping.
- increased sales by ten million dollars by end of year.
- was given added responsibility as Project Manager.

Analyzed market conditions, made recommendations and won approval for a plan to specialize efforts in power piping.

As Assistant to Vice President Marketing:

- given full responsibility to head all industrial projects including such areas as estimating, project manager, customer relations, subcontracts, engineering expediting, purchasing and cost control.
- increased sales every year since 1970.

* Personal Data:

35 years old, married, enjoy golf and sailing; active in community affairs; excellent health.

REFERENCES AND FURTHER DATA ON REQUEST

RÉSUMÉ OF A FINANCIAL EXECUTIVE

387 Western Drive   (123) 456-7890
St. Louis, Mo. (zip)

CONFIDENTIAL RESUME

of

THOMAS MELLON

FINANCIAL EXECUTIVE

***   Consistent record, with various companies, of utilization
            of financial expertise to improve earnings, increase asset
            values, establish important lines of credit. Experienced
            in all facets of financial management; in handling financial
            public relations and corporate legal matters. Extensive
            experience in public accounting, taxes, E.D.P., corporate
            financing.

***   Using sophisticated financial techniques, sound accounting
            practice, advanced management methods, turned ailing
            company into highly profitable corporation, doubling its
            listed stock value in a period of three years.

***   Restructured multi-million dollar corporation by changing
            established policies and eliminating losses after years of
            marginal operation. Accomplished outstanding turn-around
            for a third company.

***   Now employed, but seeking larger opportunity to exercise
            competence.

(FOR FURTHER DATA, PLEASE SEE FOLLOWING PAGES)

<u>1968-Present</u>   (NAME OF COMPANY ON REQUEST)

TREASURER, CHIEF FINANCIAL OFFICER, Member, Board of Directors for AMEX-listed industrial products manufacturer, with approximate annual sales of $35 million, four manufacturing plants, three warehouses. Supervise staff of 25, including Controller, Chief Accountant, Cost Accounting Manager, Manager, Inventory Control Manager.

* Responsible for all financial affairs and financial reporting of the Company, Legal liaison, **Financial Public Relations.**

* Responsibilities:

    - set up corporate budgets, departmental operating budgets, i.e.; factory overheads, R. & D., sales and G. & A. expenses; capital appropriations budget.
    - set up standard cost system and departmentalized overheads.
    - recommended profit goals as related to sales; as return on investment; measured progress by 15 relevant financial ratios.
    - calculated cash requirements, evaluated proposed capital expenditures.
    - invested cash in short-term commercial paper or otherwise as indicated currently.
    - handled Company insurance. Set up Company pension plan, secured Government approval; administered stock option and profit-sharing programs. Consulted with other officers on all compensation plans.
    - responsible for S.E.C. filings and all corporate taxes.

* Accomplishments:

    - recommended sale of and sold losing Division.
    - reduced factory costs by approximately $1 million lowering cost of goods sold from 67% of sales to 61%.
    - saved G. & A. expenses by over $1 million annually or a reduction of 37%.
    - reduced audit expenses by $80,000 annually.
    - speeded up billing and reduced receivables turnover time from 90 days to 48 days, with resulting increase of $1.5 million in cash flow.
    - earned $60,000 to $80,000 annually through short-term investments.
    - eliminated all short-term borrowing, reduced long-term debt, improved debt-equity ratio; created high credit rating.
    - increased utilization of EDP by 100% to include all corporate reporting at a cost increase of only 20%.
    - achieved Company turnaround from loss and poor credit position to annual profit after taxes of 9% and R.O.I. of over 22.7% doubling value of stock in 3 years.

* Additional Accomplishments:

    - set up sales forecasting system for Sales Department using regression analysis techniques.
    - created successful PR effort for financial community.

THOMAS MELLON   Page 3

  - reduced legal fees by $100,000 annually by handling matters within own
    competence.

<u>1966-1968</u>   SHERIDAN CANDY CORP., Hicksville, Ohio

  GENERAL MANAGER, FINANCE and ACCOUNTING, Assistant to President of $10
  million company with staff of five including Vice President-Finance, Treasurer
  and Controller.

* Administered all financial affairs of Company; by analysis of operations and effective application of financial techniques, succeeded in overcoming losses and
 achieving break-even point in first year.

  - established break-even point for products; closed out production of poor sellers.
  - established departmental budgeting that signaled loss areas, permitting correc-
    tion and reducing expenses by $25,000.
  - successfully led Company defense against attempt to unionize.

<u>1963-1966</u>   LEED CORP., Hudson, Ct.

  CONTROLLER for this manufacturer of electrical components.

* Operations much as described previously.

<u>1949-1963</u>

  Provided financial management for N. HOPPER CO., INC. (paper manufacturer),
  OVERHEAD DOORS CORP. (garage doors); worked for Certified Public Accounting
  firms.

* <u>Education</u>:

  <u>B.S.</u>, Accounting, 1949, University of Michigan.

  <u>M.B.A.</u>, Finance, 1974, University of Chicago (attending evenings).

* <u>Accreditations</u>:

  C.P.A.

* <u>Memberships</u>:

  The National Association of Financial Executives

* <u>Personal Data</u>:

  Age 49, married, one child, excellent health.

     REFERENCES AND FURTHER DATA ON REQUEST

RÉSUMÉ OF AN EDUCATIONAL ADMINISTRATOR

374 97th Boulevard   (123) 456-7890
Valley Stream, N.Y. 11580

CURRICULUM VITAE

of

DONALD ROBERTS

ADMINISTRATOR in EDUCATION

OBJECTIVE: Administrative position in educational system.

QUALIFICATIONS: Experience as Curriculum Leader, Chairman of Music Dept.,
                      Teacher with education in Science of Education, Administration
                      and Supervision, Music Education. Currently pursuing Doctoral
                      Program in Administration.

                      1973-Present   COLUMBIA UNIVERSITY, New York, N.Y.
                                      Doctoral Program: Administration.

                      1972   LONG ISLAND SCHOOL of MUSIC, L.I.U.
                                      Graduate Diploma in Music.

                      1971
                                      Graduated from Dale Carnegie Institute of Human Relations.

EDUCATION: 1970
                                      Long Island University.
                                      Professional Diploma in Administration and Supervision in
                                          Education.

                      1965
                                      M.S., Science in Education, King's College, New York,
                                          N.Y.

                      1960
                                      B.S., Music, Rutgers University, New Brunswick, N.J.
                                      Teaching Music at Elementary and Secondary levels.
                                      Graduated Cum Laude.

DONALD ROBERTS

ACCREDITATIONS: N.Y. Board of Education license no. 123456.
Certification N.Y. State Board of Regents.

EXPERIENCE: 1972-Present   P.S. 30, New York, N.Y.

Administration   CURRICULUM LEADER. Designed curriculum for grades 6, 7, 8.
Responsible for proper functioning of department including 12
teachers; assignment of classes, scheduling, budget management,
teacher training and evaluation.

                  1972   WESSINGTON HIGH SCHOOL

Teaching   VOCAL MUSIC TEACHER.

                  1966-1972   P.S. 40

                  CHAIRMAN, Music Department. Supervised teaching staff of
                  five. Responsible for:

                  - selection, training and supervision of teachers.
                  - planning and coordinating all activities in department.
Administration   - preparing and supervising budget.
                  - acting as ASSISTANT PRINCIPAL in his absence.
                  - wrote and submitted proposals for Federal funding of
                     Community Arts Program. Received funding; set up Per-
                     forming Arts program.

                  1963-1966

                  TEACHER. Taught grades 4-5 reading and arithmetic. In
                  reading used group and individual techniques including
Teaching   remedial reading as necessary. Improved reading levels more
                  than 100% above average of area schools.

                  Conducted private after-school program for underprivileged
                  children.

HOBBIES: Tennis, swimming, music.

PERSONAL DATA: Born 11/7/34, married, three children, excellent health.

REFERENCES AND FURTHER DATA ON REQUEST

RÉSUMÉ OF A PERSONNEL EXECUTIVE

37 East 59th Street   Office: (212) 123-4567
New York, N.Y. (zip)   Home: (212) 765-4321

RESUME

of

HELEN HART

PERSONNEL EXECUTIVE

***

*** After receiving Master's Degree in Sociology at the University of Chicago, employed as Stewardess by United Airlines; promoted after six months to PR and training assignments.

*** Since that time and for 12 years to present, engaged in Personnel Administration and continuing study with increasingly important responsibilities for three employers. Currently Personnel Director of $50 million manufacturing company.

*** Experienced in labor relations, new employee indoctrination programs, benefits, remuneration, job descriptions, employee review programs, security, recruiting to $50,000 annual salary level, Federal and State employment laws. Saved present employer hundreds of thousands of dollars in potential liability by instituting wage and salary increases under salary equalization program between men and women more than three years ago.

*** Invited to conduct seminar in labor relations by leading international management association. Complimented on organization and content.

*** Age 35, married, B.B.A. and M.S. degrees, excellent health.

(FOR FURTHER DATA, PLEASE SEE FOLLOWING PAGES)

HELEN HART   Page 2

EXPERIENCE:

<u>1970-Present</u>   (NAME OF COMPANY ON REQUEST), New York Area

DIRECTOR OF PERSONNEL (started as Assistant Director) for well-known manufacturer of communication equipment for industry, municipal, State and Federal
law enforcement agencies, transit authorities and the Military. Supervise staff
of ten. Report to President. Responsible for:

- recruiting, wage and salary administration, records and procedures, employee
  benefits, employee relations and social activities and plant security.
- labor relations, settlement of union grievances, participation in union contract
  negotiations; appearances before the National Labor Relations Board.
- preparation of job descriptions for all clerical, administrative and executive
  personnel.
- manpower development planning.
- budget administration.
- employee food services.
- development and improvement of work flow forms; continuing study to improve
  existing programs.

Accomplishments:

- recognized potential impact of Fair Employment Practices Act; studied job
  responsibilities and titles; upgraded female employees; avoided litigation for
  unfair practices; estimated saving to Company in potential liability of $780,000.
- credited with superior judgement in hiring middle and upper management executives to $50,000 annual remuneration.
- studied national labor scales by job classifications; recommended upgrading
  salary and piece-work rates; avoided strike in 1973 which had previously oc-
  curred during every three-year negotiation period since 1964.
- improved employee cafeteria with better food quality, attractive lounges,
  recreation area.
- conducted regular program of employee indoctrination; reduced turnover rate by
  43%.

<u>1965-1970</u>   CONTINENTAL AIRWAYS, INC., Kansas City, Mo.

MANAGER, Employee Motivation Services. Responsible for:

- in-flight and ground crew uniforms, training, motivation, grooming (3,000
  women, 2,000 men) involving Flight Attendants, Pursers, Ticket Desk,
  Passenger Assistance, Mechanics, Porters, Marketing Personnel.
- grievance hearings and settlements as possible.
- budget of $3 million.

HELEN HART   Page 3

Accomplishments:

- selected uniforms for 14 different employee categories, gained management
  approval, organized simultaneous changes for all employees and met established
  deadline. Changes previously had been accomplished in classification segments
  and were invariably late.
- set up training programs for Flight Attendants in smaller groups with superior
  results as shown by tests.
- improved employee service to public by initiating employee relations programs:
  meetings with top executives, better inter-employee communications, prizes
  recognizing exceptional service, better employee ground facilities.

<u>1963-1965</u>   LONG AIRLINES, Chicago, Ill.

TRAINING SUPERVISOR, Flight Attendants.

- set up new training program.
- conducted PR seminars throughout Greater Chicago area.

Earlier STEWARDESS (Flight Attendant) for six months.

<u>EDUCATION</u>:

<u>B.A.</u>, University of Chicago, Chicago, Ill., 1960.
Dean's List Junior and Senior years. Elected to honorary society; Homecoming
Queen.

<u>M.S.</u>, Sociology, University of Chicago, 1961.

Special courses over a period of five years (evenings) at New York University in
Personnel, Labor Relations for Non-Lawyers, Manpower Development Planning,
Laws Relating to Employment.

<u>HOBBIES</u>:

Golf, tennis, swimming, travel.

<u>PERSONAL DATA</u>:

Born 3/31/40, married, one child, excellent health.

REFERENCES AND FURTHER DATA ON REQUEST

RÉSUMÉ OF A PUBLIC ADMINISTRATOR

44 Tracay Avenue   Home (321) 098-7654
Kansas City, Mo. 12345   Office (123) 456-8765

R E S U M E

of

ROBERT SOLON

PUBLIC ADMINISTRATOR/FOUNDATION EXECUTIVE

Skilled in creating programs, setting and accomplishing goals for the alleviation
or elimination of minority group grievances by persuasion, conciliation, arbitration dealing with administrators at the highest levels of City, State and Federal
Government and with minority groups; with effective results in averting crises,
resolving disputes, developing mutual respect in confrontive situations.

	Over a period of four years hired, trained and led a professional, racially mixed staff of 30 and 12 clerical employees in the handling of conflicts, disputes, demonstrations in the North Central United States.
As Regional Director U. S. Department of Justice	Motivated staff to encourage and accomplish problem solutions by the citizens themselves in a matter of their own best self-interest.
	Established Agency liaison with Governors of various States and their staffs to use Agency programs to handle potential crises.
	Accomplished liaisons with major businesses, major Federal funding agencies and with Departments of Labor and Transportation to assure that solutions were fully understood at all levels.
	Averted riot in Detroit, Michigan by use of Department "Task Force" approach.
	Resolved school conflict in Cleveland, Ohio by coordinating administrators, teachers, community groups and students under a program that identified areas of mutual interest before attacking areas of disagreement.
As Community Relations Specialist, U. S. Dept. of Justice	Aided in averting violent confrontations in Watts area, Los Angeles, California.
	Settled conflict regarding Indian hunting and fishing

ROBERT SOLON   PAGE 2

rights in New Mexico. Chaired group to set up critical analysis of methods of solving urban problems in Newark, Paterson and Plainfield, N. J.; developed modus operandi; established training seminars for administrative officials under Federal auspices; techniques now being extensively utilized by local and State Governments.

As Trial Attorney
U. S. Dept. of
Justice

Prepared, filed and conducted civil rights cases, involving police restrictions of freedom in connection with demonstrations by large groups.

Analyzed litigation procedures and developed new procedures for expediting litigation. Worked with U. S. Supreme Court Administrative Assistant to create plans for a sub-level of jurisdiction to eliminate case overloads. Plan is under consideration.

Chronology of
Employment

1969-Present: U. S. Department of Justice, Community Relations Service

1966-1969: U. S. Department of Justice, Inter-Government Liaison Service.

1965-1966: U. S. Department of Justice, Civil Rights Division.

1962-1965:   U. S. Department of Justice, Administrative Division.

Military Service

U. S. Army, 1951-1961, Aide-de-Camp to General Symington, Tenth Combat Division, Vietnam.

Education

L. L. B., Harvard University School of Law, Cambridge, Mass.

B. A., Political Science, University of Denver, Denver, Colo.

Accrediations

Member of the Bar, District of Columbia, Maryland and Virginia.

Personal data

Age 39, married, three children, excellent health.

REFERENCES AND FURTHER DATA ON REQUEST

RÉSUMÉ OF A RETAIL EXECUTIVE

37 Robe Boulevard
Pasadena, Cal. (zip)

Home: (123) 456-7890
Business: (123) 654-3210

RESUME

of

TAYLOR GIMBEL

RETAIL EXECUTIVE/DIVISIONAL MERCHANDISE MANAGER/STORE MANAGER

==

***   Progressive and successful career in retailing
from Trainee to Merchandise Manager with
major Los Angeles department store.

***   Record of efficient departmental reorganiza-
tions, consistent volume increases; innovative
promotional ideas, new display and packaging
concepts.

***   Develop buyer confidence and find strategies
to maximize profits and volume.

(FOR FURTHER DATA, PLEASE SEE FOLLOWING PAGES)

BUSINESS EXPERIENCE:

1966-Present   WILSHIRE DEPARTMENT STORES, Los Angeles, Cal.,
                                internationally known $1 billion plus department store
                                retailer with branches in major metropolitan areas.

1973-Present, MERCHANDISE MANAGER, Pasadena, Cal., with additional assignment as Supervisor of $24 million branch store. Responsible for:

- merchandising Major Appliances, Television, Radios and Stereo Sound Studio,
  Air Conditioners, Housewares, Budget Store, Auto Shop; with departmental
  sales of $10 million.

Examples of Accomplishments:

- overcame poor sales of T.V.'s, stereo systems and service contracts.
- changed location, improved display with new display concept, improved product emphasis and sales presentation; increased sales 27% in first year (20%
  over plan and best increase among all branches).
- surmounted loss of housewares space reduced 40%,by better identification of
  potential best sellers, placing orders accordingly, conceiving new display
  presentation; increased sales 12% above plan, and only 15% below previous
  year in larger space.

Jun. 1972-May 1973, MERCHANDISE MANAGER, San Diego, Cal. for Leisure Living,
Housewares, Budget Store, Toys, Auto Shop.

Examples of Accomplishments:

- developed new floor plan for poorly organized Housewares Department; created
  new displays, impulse shopping atmosphere, improved traffic flow. Major
  elements of plan were adopted as proto-types for all Wilshire stores; increased
  Fall sales 13% in first year (10% above plan), the highest percentage increase
  among all departments and stores in Division. Increased spring sales 9%,
  second largest Housewares increase among all stores.
- for entire departmental responsibilities achieved first, second or third best
  percentage increases among all stores.

Jan. 1971-Jan. 1972, MERCHANDISE MANAGER, Long Beach, Cal. for Men's Store,
Silver, Luggage, Cameras, Fine Jewelry.

- increased volume 7%.

July 1969-Feb. 1971, BUYER, Men's Underwear, Hosiery, Handkerchiefs and
Scarves, Los Angeles, Cal.

- started new trend in men's accessories; imported new and different products
  from Europe; created $100,000 new volume in six months.

TAYLOR GIMBEL   Page 3

- conceived handkerchiefs promotion based on new approach; used with great success by manufacturer nationally after Wilshire introduction.
- designed new men's underwear display fixture now used in all stores.

1966-1969   BUYER, Men's Underwear and Hosiery, Main Store

- originated theme "Look as Well Inside as Outside"; sold $27,000 in three days.
- rated most profitable Buyer for Company 1968.
- gave vendors responsibility for departmental mark-on percentages.
- appointed Chairman, Corporate Buying Committee.

1958-1966   MEYER AND DANIELS, Portland, Oregon

July 1966-Dec. 1966   BUYER, Men's Shirts, Hosiery, Pajamas, Robes

1964-1966   BUYER, Men's Dress Shirts, Hosiery

- created unique promotion still used by Company; at first promotion sold entire stock in one day.
- achieved departmental net profit of 20.5%.
- increased volume from $4 million to $6 million in one year.

June 1963-Feb. 1964   BUYER, Appliances

1958-1963   Successively Trainee, Head of Stock, Assistant Buyer, Associate Buyer.

MILITARY SERVICE: U. S. NAVY, Shore Patrol, 1956-1958

EDUCATION: B. A., History and Business Administration, University of California at Los Angeles.

                       Ph. B., Political Science and Philosophy, 1955.

                       Certificate, Stanford University of Retailing, 1960.

PUBLICATIONS: "What's Wrong with Housewares," Housewares Magazine

                       "Merchandise Review," Men's Furnishings.

                       "Merchandise Review," Men's Underwear.

HOBBIES: All sports, hiking, travel.

PERSONAL DATA: Born 2/15/34, married, two children, excellent health. Willing to relocate.

REFERENCES AND FURTHER DATA ON REQUEST

RÉSUMÉ OF A MERCHANDISER

347 Miller Avenue   Home: (123) 456-7890
Detroit, Mich. (zip)   Office: (321) 098-7654

RESUME

of

WILLIAM WANAMAKER

BUYER

Branch Merchandiser

Store Manager

*** Excellent record as productive, profit-oriented, aggressive, fashion-aware Buyer, with history of volume building in one of America's leading stores with 10 branches; increased mark-ups.

*** Creative in display and product presentation, promotion planning; effective in departmental organization, advance budgeting, sales training; work well with all levels of personnel to achieve maximum results. Hold daily sales meetings. Maintain quality, style image.

*** Experienced in wide variety of department store merchandise classifications; with record of rapid promotion from Executive Training Program.

(FOR FURTHER DATA, PLEASE SEE FOLLOWING PAGES)

WILLIAM WANAMAKER   Page 2

<u>1962-Present</u>   DAYTON CROWLEY CO., Detroit, Mich.

BUYER, SHOE SALON (1970-1972). Responsible for main store and ten branches, supervising three junior executives, six departmental assistants and fifteen to eighteen sales people, and volume of nearly $5 million.

- maintain close contacts with all fashion trends, designers, manufacturers to maintain leader image of this high fashion specialty store.
- project high-fashion environment in departmental displays, windows, advertising, publicity, and public relations.
- efficiently administer administrative details resulting in consistently accurate inventories, reduced mark-downs, improved turnover.
- gave increased attention to branch stores and stocks; created sales increases of 22%.
- conduct daily sales meeting with selling personnel re customer presentations, new lines, advertising, fashion trends as applicable.
- increased overall sales 37% and mark-ups by 4%.

BUYER, Men's Nightwear (1966-1970), estimated volume was approximately $1.2 million. At end of first year, sales volume was $3 million; at end of second year $3.5 million, and continuing to grow up to time of transfer to shoes. Responsibilities and actions similar to those described above.

<u>1964-1966</u>, ASSISTANT BUYER, Boy's Wear.

<u>1963-1964</u>, ASSISTANT BUYER, Fabrics.

<u>1962-1963</u>, ASSISTANT BUYER, Jewelry.

<u>1962</u>, ASSISTANT BUYER, House Furnishings.

<u>MILITARY SERVICE</u>:

<u>1959-1961</u>   U.S. ARMY (in Europe)

<u>EDUCATION</u>:

<u>1954-1958</u>   Princeton University, B.A., History of Art Major.

<u>PERSONAL DATA</u>:

Age 35, married, willing to relocate.

REFERENCES AND FURTHER DATA ON REQUEST

Useful Words and Phrases

There are certain words that may help you to express yourself better and phrases and sentences typical of the succinct and vivid language of a résumé. The examples given below are intended only to guide you and to suggest style. Appraise them carefully before choosing a word or phrase that fits you best. Your résumé should be as distinctive as are your fingerprints.

ABOUT YOUR EXPERIENCE

consistent record (of progress, growth, achievements, promotion)

demonstrably (successful, capable, effective)

effective

experienced

extensive

intensive

in-depth, comprehensive, of wide scope, wide, broad, diversified, varied

intimate (familiarity with rules, regulations, procedures)

progressive

solid

complete

thoroughgoing

successful

ABOUT YOU

accustomed, used to	contest or award winner
an administrator	contributor
analytical	contributory
broad gauge	controlled
(possess) communication skills	a coordinator
competent, capable, able	dedicated

developer

distinguished

dynamic

educated, schooled, trained

efficient, effective

exceptional (avoid
"unexceptionable")

an executive

a generalist

harmonious

imaginative, conceptual

indoctrinated (with)

ingenious, inventive

talented

innovative, creative

a leader

a manager

motivated

a motivator

multilingual, bilingual

a negotiator

an organizer

outstanding

planner

a producer

reliable

responsible

skilled

a specialist

strategist

stress resistant

student of

a supervisor

a trainee

a trainer

traveled

ABOUT YOUR SKILLS AND ABILITIES

analyze

assist

communicate

conceive (an idea)

contribute

create

create profit, profitability

delegate

develop

economize, save money

implement

innovate

learn

lead

organize, systematize, install

plan

qualify for

recruit

solve problems

supervise, manage, administer

train, indoctrinate, teach

understand

work well with others, work in harmony

write, compose, create copy

ABOUT YOUR ACCOMPLISHMENTS

accomplished

achieved

achieved company or division
   turnaround

contributed

increased, multiplied profit

increased, multiplied sales

introduced new concepts

progressed

reduced, expanded

reorganized

restored profit

saved

sold

succeeded

In the examples below these words and phrases are put to work.

Comprehensively trained in every aspect of procedures.

Product student, market researcher, competition evaluator, sales planner, salesman.

Competent in developing existing customers; in finding new customers; in implementing sales plans; in maintaining customer loyalty.

Single, young, motivated, willing to travel, willing to relocate.

Accomplished in organizing efficient production, in production control planning, and in the effective utilization of the complete range of metal fabricating equipment.

Able to bring effective solutions to complex (mechanical, engineering, financial, marketing, pricing) problems.

Willing to undertake training. Capable of learning. Possess imagination to conceive goals and find ways to accomplish them, quality of leadership, and ability to communicate.

Author of program to expedite critical data to management leading to expansion (other).

Proven skill in defining requirements, procedures, methods, display, and report formats to keep management informed of progress.

Experienced in managing salesmen, training, recruiting, sales planning, utilizing all techniques (audiovisual, flip charts, advertising, contests, tie-ins, advance merchandising) to stimulate sales.

Labor intensive, capital intensive (industry).

Experienced recruiter and trainer of top producers in the industry, consistently sought by competitive firms because of known qualities of leadership and ability to communicate and identify with others.

Ability to analyze and reorganize corporate administrative procedures and use advanced techniques (word processing, communications center, electronic data processing) to achieve greater efficiency at lower cost.

Talent for recognizing better ways to accomplish business objectives through coordination, consolidation, systematization, retraining.

Able to see interdisciplinary relationships and express them effectively.

Credited with novel concepts and creative approaches to the production of scores of recognized 30 and 60 second prime-time TV spot commercials for leading national advertisers.

After 15 years in public service interested in making a career change to the private sector and qualified in personnel, college administration, recruiting, manpower development, general administration.

Six years of secretarial and other office experience as receptionist, book-keeper, filing clerk, and PBX operator with a variety of service companies: law firm, management consultant, insurance company, advertising agency. Type accurately 60 to 65 words per minute, with skills increasing continuously.

Awareness of legal needs of business and ability to provide clear answers and effective remedies for corporate legal problems.

Broad administrative background as senior executive with giant public authority; special expertise in the planning and operation of major seaports and transportation centers. Competent in negotiation, persuasion, leadership, and motivation. Record of consistent promotion to greater responsibilities throughout career.

Intimately familiar with U.S. markets, business methods, requirements, strategies. Record of creating sales and profits of significant proportions, measured in millions of dollars in diverse industries involving marketing to supermarkets, chains, department stores, government agencies, institutions, wholesalers, using brokers, agents, direct salesmen.

Comprehensively trained and experienced in brokerage and investment banking, in both "front office" and "back office" procedures: portfolio management, daily transactions and administration, cash flow management, Exchange and S.E.C. compliance. Record of profit contributions to employers.

Experienced in establishing effective management information systems; in the expanded use of E.D.P. to provide critical data expeditiously; in cost accounting, inventory control, production control; in reducing lead time; in measuring productivity; in creating controls at all levels of production to identify profit leaks; in applying innovative methods of accomplishing corporate objectives and increased profitability.

Talent for analysis and organization of complex administrative problems. Innovative. Enthusiastic. Ability to train others. Record of important contributions in management, timesaving systems and profit to major multimillion and billion dollar corporations. Record of conscientious application, reliability and loyalty in every position held and ready acceptance or responsibility to get improved results in every assignment.

Experienced in most aspects of insurance, with emphasis in the investigative and adjusting field, which includes extensive legal negotiations, with autonomous discretion from major insurance companies to settle cases at the highest levels. Also general brokerage experience, including solicitation and development of accounts, counseling relative to insurance needs, complex underwriting evaluations, and placement of coverages by various carriers.

Accustomed to complete management responsibilities for accounting and controls, front office, food and beverage, golf course, club house, entertainment, and other facilities; and to financial reporting, profit and cash flow projections; planning and development. Accomplished also in developing convention business, arranging entertainment, providing gourmet food service and high level of other services. Experienced in close analysis of operating figures and correction of trouble areas; in the use of E.D.P. to assist the managerial function.

Successful record as president of own business; formerly director of industrial engineering for multimillion dollar corporation. Experienced in the selection and evaluation of capital equipment needs, production control, rate setting, productivity standards and measurement, systems and procedures, plant layout, incentive plans; in power plant operation.

Record of major contributions in increased revenues, cost savings; in leadership and revitalization of underproductive departments; in research, analysis, and recommendations with respect to feedstocks, tankage, storage, production and marketing optimization, cost control, economics, forecasting, budgeting.

Successful career as financial analyst, securities salesman, knowledgeable in all areas of brokerage including municipal bonds, commodities, underwritings, placements, individual and corporate portfolio management. Competent trainer, leader, developer of manpower. Excellent public speaker, widely experienced in conducting seminars and adult education courses in securities and investment.

Expert in marketing wide range of ethical and proprietary pharmaceuticals and complex electronic health instrumentation products, with in-depth knowledge of markets, sales techniques, training methods. Skilled in communications. Numerous company awards for sales and other achievements. Accustomed to leading, training, and motivating large staffs and hundreds of employees.

Leader and developer of sales personnel for effective administration of greater responsibilities.

Expert in accommodating promotion programs to regional, trade, and consumer characteristics; in developing innovative packaging to enhance consumer response.

Ability to see what needs to be done, to do it or get it done in a general management capacity.

Exceptionally consistent record of turning loss-operated companies into profitmakers; recently increased sales and production fourfold in less than three years.

Ability to conceptualize and implement broad, complex programs to reach new goals.

Effective market researcher, sales leader, and trainer with expertise in all kinds of packaging and creative sales ideas.

Complete knowledge of the application of graphics to good design with ability to curtail cost.

Demonstrated management ability in national marketing with strong following among chains, discounters, distributors; excellent personal salesman.

School psychologist and counselor, self-starting and innovative.

Record of continuous promotion to positions of greater responsibility; currently holding P.&L. responsibility for multimillion dollar division where sales have tripled and a profit objective has been met. Fully equipped in all aspects of management; in developing management information systems; in full utilization of data processing; in long-range planning and implementation.

Comprehensive experience in the financial and administrative management of huge engineering and construction projects overseas and in the United States involving diverse heavy industrial and military installations; assured their profitable completion.

Extensive educational background and practical experience in human relations, the latter as program developer for nonprofit organization working in South Africa to improve the effectiveness of the organization's structures, human relations, and economic and health conditions of the nationals of Tanzania and Kenya; and of the organization's personnel. Conceived program and assigned to implement it.

A P P E N D I X   C

Job Responsibilities in Major Job Classifications

You may find it helpful to review the activities in certain job classifications. The list below does not include *all* job responsibilities.

Not all companies specify the same responsibilities. R.&D. as well as warehousing and shipping may sometimes be assigned to marketing and sometimes elsewhere. As a vice-president of marketing you would be expected to be familiar with all the elements listed under that heading depending on a company's organizational structure. As a sales manager you would be responsible only for the areas shown under that heading. You will get ideas about other responsibilities, such as product manager, from one or more of the résumés reproduced.

The classifications include most of the duties within the major functions of a company: marketing, finance, and production. Select your area of activity within these categories.

The list also includes personnel, purchasing, retail, data processing, and others selected somewhat arbitrarily; it could have been expanded ad infinitum. We wished to show that, whatever the job classification, your résumé should discuss the responsibilities and accomplishments normally associated with that job. A sales manager, for example, must know the markets of the industry in question.

Use this section as a reminder of your responsibilities, so that you do not omit relevant and important activities with which you should be familiar.

ACCOUNTING

Act as cashier
Adjust entries
Age accounts receivable and accounts payable
Analyze intercompany expenses
Approve petty cash and checks
Bank reconciliations
Budgets, forecasts, and financial planning
Closing entries

Collect from debtors; pay creditors

Consolidate reports for parent company with recommendations as to standing and results of operations of local branches

Correspondence

Dispose promotional items

Examine salesmen's collections and promotional remittances

Examine weekly reports of branch managers and regional offices

Footings

Maintain books of original entry, general ledger, and subsidiary ledgers

Maintain records and control costs of inventory

Posting to the general ledger

Prepare regular payroll

Prepare reversing entries

Prepare taxes

Prepare various supporting schedules

Take off and post closing trial balance

Trial balance

AUDITING

Age receivables and payables

Analysis and evaluation of cash flow, fiscal and interim statements, and projected statements

Analytical audit of books of original entry and records

Analyze turnovers of receivables and payables

Cash counts

Close books

Comparative analysis of sales and financial statements between two or more fiscal periods

Compute breakeven inventory, estimated inventory, and estimated profit or loss

Conduct physical inventory

Confer with company's officers and accountants

Continuous reconciliations

Detailed analysis of balance sheet and P.&L

Evaluate D.&B. ratings

Examine and check other audit reports

Examine bonds, stocks, important documents, contracts

Examine canceled checks and checks being held

Examine notes

Examine shipping documents

Examine pension fund, welfare fund, vacation fund, unemployment fund, education fund, accrual fund

Examine taxes

Financial and accounting analysis of diversified multidivisional corporations

Observe factory inventory flow and operations

Post to general ledger

Prepare entries; journal, adjusting, correcting, reversing

Prepare financial statements with opinions

Prepare, present, discuss, explain reports

Prepare taxes

Prepare various schedules

Send out trade checks and verification

Systems suggestions

Take off trial balance and post closing trial balance

Work on books of original entry

DATA PROCESSING

Applications to inventory, production, accounts receivable, accounts payable, payroll, sales, shipping, order processing

Budgets

Data centers

Diagnostic systems

Econometric models

Economic models

Educational systems

Forecasting

Hardware, selection of

Leased time

Management information systems

Minicomputer use

Models—financial, marketing, production

Procedural manuals

Programming

Real time

Scientific systems   Training
Softwear, selection of   Utilization, maximum

FINANCE

Acceleration of financial reporting
Accounting
Acquisitions and mergers
Audits and controls
Balance sheets
Bank reconciliations
Bank relationships
Budgets
Capital resource planning
Cash flow
Cash handling
C.P.A. accreditation
Chart of accounts
Compensation
Consolidations
Cost analysis
Credits and collections—bad debt ratios, accounts receivable, aging
Economic correlations
E.D.P. systems
Financing
Financial models
Financial public relations
Financial reporting
Forecasting
Foreign currency fluctuation
Insurance
Inventory control, turnover
Investment
Invoicing systems
Long range planning
Management information systems

Negotiations
New York Stock Exchange, AMEX reports
New York Stock Exchange, AMEX listings
Pensions, fringe benefits, profit sharing plans
Pricing formulas
Profit and loss reporting
Profitability
S.E.C. reports, registrations, prospectuses
Staff training
Taxes
Terms of sale
Training
Underwritings

MARKETING

Sales management
  Budget
  Compensation
  District sales
  Expenses
  Field sales
  Incentives
  Markets
  National sales
  Organization
  Quotas
  Regional sales
  Sales meetings
  Sales planning
  Sales training
  Territory routing
Sales promotion
  Brochures
  Budget
  Circulars
  Direct mail
  Display
  Merchandising
  Packaging
  Presentations
  Promotions
Public relations
  Budget
  Employee public relations
  Media liaison
  Planning
  Press releases
  Speechwriting
Legal liaison
  Advertising agreements
  Co-op advertising, discounts, pricing
  Sherman antitrust
Computer utilization

Planning
Product management
(marketing in microcosm)
Research and development
  Budget
  Market evaluations
  New products
  Obsolescence
  Old products
  Product evaluation
  Quality comparisons
Advertising
  Agency relations
  Budgets
  Contests

Copy, copy testing
Legal liaison
  Media: print, TV, radio
Production
Themes
Market research
  Cost projections
  Demography
  Market testing
  New market planning
  Pricing
Forecasting
Pricing (pricing for profit)
Warehousing and shipping
(distribution)

PERSONNEL, INDUSTRIAL RELATIONS, AND MANPOWER DEVELOPMENT

Administration, wage and salary
Arbitrations
Bonding
Budget
Community relations
Computer utilization
Credit unions
Disability
Discipline
Employee orientation
Employee public relations
Employee productivity reviews
Fair Employment Practices Act
Food service
Grievances
Group insurance
Hiring

Interviewing
Job description
Labor negotiations
Legal liaison
Loans
Major medical insurance
Manpower development
Manpower planning
Medical department
Morale
National Labor Relations Board
OSHA (Occupational Safety and
Health Administration) compliance
Policy and procedure
Records
Security
Social functions

Training programs
Unemployment compensation
Unemployment insurance

Welfare and pension plans
Workmen's compensation

PRODUCTION

Automatic equipment
Automation
Budgets
Chemical engineering
Civil engineering
Computer utilization
Construction
Conveyorization
Cost control
Electrical engineering
Electronics engineering
Environment
Industrial engineering
Inventory control
Manpower planning
Mechanical engineering
Metallurgy
New construction, startup
Patents

Personnel
Plant layout
Power
Production control, scheduling, planning, flow
Purchasing, materials management
Quality control
Quality engineering
Recruiting
Research and development
Space planning
Stampings, forgings, castings, extrusions
Safety engineering
Systems
Tools and dies
Training
Warehousing and shipping
Waste disposal, recycling

PURCHASING AND MATERIAL MANAGEMENT

Alternate option purchasing
Blanket and annual contracts
Budget
Computer utilization
Economic Order Quantity
(EOQ) purchasing
Economics
Environment
Inventory control

Legal liaison
Make or buy
Market studies
Packaging
Price trend analysis
Shortages
Strikes
Turnover
Value analysis

RETAIL

Acquisition	Management information systems
Administration	Market analysis
Advertising	Market changes
Branch store administration,	Markup, mark-on
expansion	Merchandise selection
Budgeting	Merchandising
Buying	Open-to-buy
Cash flow	Operations
Computer utilization	Promotion
Credit	Quality control
Department layout	Retailing mathematics
Display	Receiving
Expansion	Security
Financial planning	Shipping
Financial reporting	Staffing
Housekeeping	Store layout
Inventory control	Systems
Leadership	Training

A P P E N D I X   D

Professional Résumé
Services

Like doctors, lawyers, and advertising agencies, professional résumé services do excellent, mediocre, or poor work. It is therefore important to select your professional résumé service carefully.

In addition to résumé writing, a résumé service may perform the following tasks:

Reproduction
Mailing

Supplying mailing lists—custom and standard
Broadcast letter writing
Interview technique assistance
Aptitude testing
Psychological testing
Third party services
Organization of complete job campaigns
Corporate "out placement"
Executive search
Career counseling
Compensation guidance

Though some consider professionally prepared résumés to lack the stamp of personality evident in a "homemade" résumé, many successful leaders in business, the professions, and the arts have used them. Writing is a difficult task, requiring practice and a knowledge of the rules. Writing about yourself can be even more difficult. You might wish to employ a professional writer for the following reasons:

You have been unable to organize your employment history.
You find the task of writing about yourself tedious and exasperating.
You cannot express "you" in a way that you like.
You speak better than you write.
You have neither the time nor the patience to write your own résumé.
You cannot decide what to omit and what to include.
Your experience is narrow.
You don't know whether your experience is narrow or comprehensive with respect to the job you want.

Ask the professional résumé service to show you samples of their work. Arrange to meet the individual who will be writing your résumé.

The cost of a résumé varies with the time and expertise required to write it. In a large city such as New York the prices will range from $50 for a single page résumé to $400 for a complex one. Like any business, your résumé service has such overhead expenses as rent, heat, light, taxes, and secretarial help. Preparing a résumé involves its planning, writing and rewriting, proofreading, interviewing, and researching reference material. Fees of $50 an hour are about the minimum needed to run a professional résumé service in a large urban center. The following typical fees for a professionally written résumé are based on information supplied by six résumé writing firms:

By mail
   $25 to $75
   $50 per page (maximum: $150)
   $50 per page (no maximum)

By personal interview
   $50 per page
   $85 for first page, $35 for second page, and $25 for third page
   $36 to $60 per hour
   New entrant to job market: $35 to $50
   Clerical: $50 to $75
   Lower middle management executive: $100
   Upper middle management executive: $150
   Vice-president for small company: $200
   Vice-president for large company: $250
   Chief executive officer or president: $300 to $350

A professional résumé writer usually provides a résumé that is ready for use as far as its content is concerned, but requires retyping in camera ready form for reproduction. Those résumé services that have their own printing equipment include the cost of typing in their printing cost of the first 100 copies per page. The typing and printing costs shown below are taken from a survey of eight companies. Quality of printing and paper, accuracy and speed of typing (an experienced résumé typist requires less time than a novice), résumé layout—all affect the cost and all are difficult to assess except based on the firm's reputation.

100 copies per page, $3.50 (typing free); 200 copies per page, $5.00
100 copies per page, $4.90 (typing free)
Typing $5 per page
Typing $8 to $10 per page (public stenographer, New York City)
Typing $8 per hour (public stenographer, suburban area)
Typing $11 per hour (experienced résumé typist, New York City)
100 copies per page, first 100: $10 to $14 depending on quality of paper
Additional copies: $3.00 per 100 per page

Index